Designing Judicial Review

Designing Judicial Review

Interest Groups, Congress,
and Communications Policy

Charles R. Shipan

Ann Arbor

The University of Michigan Press

Copyright © by the University of Michigan 1997
All rights reserved
Published in the United States of America by
The University of Michigan Press
Manufactured in the United States of America
⊗ Printed on acid-free paper

2000   1999   1998   1997   4   3   2   1

A CIP catalog record for this book is available from the British Library.

Library of Congress Cataloging-in-Publication Data

Shipan, Charles R., 1961–
    Designing judicial review : interest groups, Congress, and
  communications policy / Charles R. Shipan.
        p.   cm.
    Includes bibliographical references and index.
    ISBN 0-472-10703-8 (cloth : acid-free paper)
    1. Judicial review—United States.   I. Title.
  KF4575.S54   1997
  347.73'12—dc21   97-4658
                                                        CIP

For Kathy

Contents

Acknowledgments

A commonly held perception is that research is a solitary pursuit. Fortunately, however, I can attest that my work on this project was anything but solitary. At every stage of the project I benefited from the encouragement, advice, and criticism of my colleagues, and I am delighted to finally be able to acknowledge their wonderful generosity. While their encouragement and advice were always more fun to receive, their criticism undoubtedly improved and helped shape the final product.

Because this project had its foundations in work conducted at Stanford University, I would like to begin my thanks by acknowledging the guidance and influence of John Ferejohn and Roger Noll. Both were instrumental in helping me get started and in ensuring that I finished. Others at Stanford whom I would like to acknowledge for various combinations of support, counsel, and friendship include Bill Lowry, Dave Fallek, Catherine Shapiro, Marty Finnemore, David Brady, Keith Krehbiel, and Dick Brody. Finally, I would like to acknowledge the financial support of the Markle Foundation and the Center for Economic Policy Research at Stanford.

I was fortunate to spend one year working on this project as a research fellow at the Brookings Institution. Forrest Maltzman, John Chubb, Matthew Palmer, and Wally Mullin generously read and commented on various sections of the work, and Kent Weaver and Tom Mann helped provide a stimulating environment in which to conduct research. I have similarly benefited from the scholarly environment at the University of Iowa and wish to acknowledge in particular Jim Lindsay, Sally Kenney, and Pev Squire, all of whom provided encouragement and advice during the preparation of this manuscript.

Four other scholars deserve special thanks for reading—and rereading—parts of the manuscript and providing me with the benefit of their insights. These four are Ron Cass, Bob Katzmann, Kathy Bawn, and Shep Melnick. Their suggestions helped me focus every aspect of this project, improving it immeasurably, and I benefited immensely from their wide-ranging intellects. I am deeply grateful to them for their time and efforts.

Finally, the most important contributions came from people who haven't read a word of this book. My mother, Betty Shipan, has always been remarkably supportive of my academic endeavors. My two children—Jeffrey, who was born as I was working on the first draft, and Rebecca, who was born as I was finishing the final draft, have provided me with joy and inspiration beyond what I could have imagined. And my wife, Kathy Malville-Shipan, has been, to quote a friend of ours, a shining star. Whatever I have accomplished is due in large part to her incredible support and love. It is to her that this book is dedicated.

Figures

Tables

CHAPTER 1

Introduction: Judicial Review as a Political Variable

Political actors are well aware that current choices constrain future choices and greatly affect future outcomes. Therefore, when passing laws, goal-oriented actors pay a great deal of attention to the "details" of legislation, including the structural and procedural details. Examples of battles over these types of details abound, especially regarding the use of structures and procedures to plan and account for bureaucratic actions. Debates during the creation of the Interstate Commerce Commission represent a paradigmatic example of such a battle (Skowronek 1982; Fiorina 1986). Similarly, Moe (1989) has outlined the disputes over structure during the creation of the Environmental Protection Agency, the Occupational Safety and Health Administration, and the Consumer Product Safety Commission. And McCubbins, Noll, and Weingast (1989) have described the primacy of procedural details in the 1977 amendments to the Clean Air Act.[1] At the root of all these battles is the awareness that structures and procedures matter.

In this study I provide a detailed look at another way procedures matter by examining how political actors attempt to plan for court involvement in policy decisions. More specifically, I focus on the use of judicial review provisions in regulatory legislation as a means of gaining political advantage. At the same time, by focusing on the politics surrounding the inclusion in legislation of specific provisions for judicial review, I also seek to add to our understanding of the role that courts play in policy-making.

Courts in the Political System

While courts have always been an integral part of the political process, they have not always been viewed as being *political*. A major exception to

---

1. See also West's 1985 investigation of the introduction of rule-making procedures into the Federal Trade Commission's decision-making process and Owen and Braeutigam's 1978 analysis of the strategic use of process. On the general theme of political actors having preferences over institutions, see Knott and Miller 1987.

this perspective comes from the field of judicial behavior, where the courts have received an explicitly political foundation from the attitudinal model.[2] This model, which holds that judges have policy preferences and vote according to these preferences, has been used to explore a variety of topics, such as the granting of certiorari and opinion assignments within the Supreme Court.[3]

Viewing the courts as political actors is no longer the sole province of the attitudinal model. Students of political institutions increasingly have begun to incorporate courts into their models and explanations of political events. Several studies, for example, explicitly have addressed the political role played by the courts in the formation of public policy.[4] Positive theorists also have turned their attention to the courts with increasing regularity in recent years, modeling the interaction between courts and other political institutions.[5] And a few studies of specific policy areas have even inspected the debates over the inclusion of specific provisions for judicial review.[6]

While many studies have begun to examine the interaction between courts and other political actors and institutions, several aspects of the courts' role remain underexamined. For example, why are the courts reviewing agency actions in the first place? Once the courts are involved, what types of actions can they take? Do they have free reign to alter policy in any manner they desire? Or are their decisions and actions circumscribed? To what extent, and under what conditions, do other actors try to limit (or expand) the role the courts play? What influences are significant in determining the answers to these other questions?

There are at least two ways one can approach these questions. The first can be labeled the *traditional* model.[7] In this model, judicial review is

---

2. Another major exception, of course, is the line of work spawned by Dahl (1957).

3. A comprehensive statement and investigation of the attitudinal model can be found in Segal and Spaeth 1993. See also Pritchett 1948; Schubert 1965; Rohde and Spaeth 1976; and Segal and Cover 1989.

4. Some of the best examples include Melnick 1983, 1994; Katzmann 1986; Shapiro 1988; and Rosenberg 1991. See also Thernstrom 1987, but note the stinging review by Karlan and McCrary (1988).

5. This literature is growing rapidly. Early studies include Marks 1988; Ferejohn and Shipan 1988, 1990; Ferejohn and Weingast 1992; Gely and Spiller 1990; and Spiller and Gely 1992. Several legal scholars have also turned their attention to this area, including Eskridge (1991a, 1991b), Eskridge and Ferejohn (1992), Farber and Frickey (1988, 1991), Mashaw (1990), and Spitzer (1990). Studies that merge the attitudinal model and positive theory include Cameron, Cover, and Segal 1990 and Segal, Cameron, and Cover 1992.

6. Most notably, see Light's 1992 informative description of review provisions regarding actions of the Veterans Administration, and Melnick 1983, esp. 7–8 and 373–79; 1994.

7. This model corresponds to what Mashaw (1990) labels "judicial idealism" and is also related to what Segal and Spaeth denote the "legal model." See also the informative

almost a given. Debate generally focuses on normative issues—for example, whether court action is appropriate, what actions or decisions courts should require of bureaucracies, and what factors and ideals should underlie court decisions. A typical question is whether it is *proper* for courts to act; that they can act if they so choose is rarely, if ever, questioned.

A closely related focus of studies in this vein is on what the purpose of courts should be. A representative example is provided by Choper (1980), who, in his insightful analysis of the function of the Supreme Court, contends that the essential role of judicial review is to protect fundamental rights.[8] Stewart's 1975 critical review of the development of administrative law strikes a similar chord—the traditional model, he points out, argues that the primary goals of the courts are the protection of private autonomy and the provision of additional assurance that agencies do not exceed their authorized powers. Another related argument is made by Ely (1980), who advances the normative contention that the role of the courts is to ensure the proper functioning of the democratic system. Yet another view is proffered by Rose-Ackerman (1992), who argues that courts should improve the democratic accountability of agency policy-making by requiring agencies to take into account the costs and benefits of a policy action on all citizens.[9]

Implicit in this approach is a stylized view of the judiciary's role in the political process. First, Congress delegates policy-making responsibility to an agency; second, the agency chooses a policy; and finally, the courts review the policy choice, seeking to make sure administrative action was appropriate. Most notably, in this model the stages, especially the first and third stages, are regarded as distinct from each other. Congress decides whether or not to delegate decision-making authority; the agency then decides, within certain boundaries, what action to take; and finally, the courts make sure the agency action falls within the proper bounds. As far as the courts are concerned, the main focus is on issues like justice, fairness, liberty, and protection from the state. While Congress may be concerned with setting proper boundaries and broad policy goals for the

---

discussion in Cass 1986 about dominant strands of thought that run through writings on administrative law. For a comparison of the legal model with models that incorporate more political factors, see Segal and Spaeth 1993 and T. George and L. Epstein 1992.

8. Like many scholars who work in this vein, Choper focuses on constitutional rather than statutory issues. This tendency was observed by Russell: "To an English common law lawyer judicial review refers primarily to judicial review of administrative actions. . . . Nowadays when political scientists and constitutional lawyers talk about judicial review it is not this older, more generic use of the term that they have in mind" (1991, 116).

9. A discussion of some of these approaches can be found in Clinton 1989, which, along with Wolfe 1994 and Lasser 1988, reevaluates the foundations and development of judicial review.

agency, at the same time Congress pays little attention to what will happen once the courts enter the process.[10]

An alternative view—a more *political* model—presents a quite different list of considerations. This view follows from developments in positive theory that accentuate the significance of procedure and structure as means to garnering and securing political advantage (McCubbins, Noll, and Weingast 1987, 1989; Moe 1989, 1990a, 1990b; Horn and Shepsle 1989; Macey 1992a, 1992b; Shepsle 1992). In these accounts, actors realize that they are involved a sequential game. In other words, they are forward-looking and they consider the future benefits that derive from each current action. Provisions chosen during the writing of laws, such as those concerning judicial review, are not "merely" procedural, as these provisions will likely affect the potential range of actions available to actors in the future. Such consideration of provisions occurs not only with the bureaucracy, as the aforementioned studies have demonstrated, but also with the judiciary. Because of this recognition of the future importance of current procedural choices, the phases of the policy-making process no longer can be viewed as distinct. Instead, politics is introduced into judicial review by virtue of consideration of review provisions in the first stage.

These two views yield dissimilar hypotheses about how political actors behave. In the first account, court action is something that happens "later"—no attention is paid to the possibility that actors will expect and try to plan ahead for court action. Therefore, actors simply will view the courts as adding another layer of insurance against improper or unfair agency actions. Arguments generally will not take place over the exact specification of judicial review provisions, and those that do will be concerned with procedural ways of ensuring fidelity to these values and others, such as individual liberty and private autonomy.[11]

The alternative view presents a considerably different picture of what happens in the first stage, or what I call the *front end,* of the policy process. Interest groups and members of Congress know that details of procedure and structure are important—to paraphrase Moe (1990a), procedural pol-

---

10. This approach is common to public-administration scholars as well as legal scholars. Even so astute an observer of administration as Robert Cushman (1941) devoted very little space in his magisterial account of regulatory agencies to the legislative specification of review provisions. More recently, in their excellent administrative law textbook, Carter and Harrington have written, "As a practical matter Congress usually says nothing about reviewability of administrative decisions in authorizing legislation. The statutory language that does exist often reiterates APA language and/or *Abbott Labs's* presumption of reviewability" (1991, 355).

11. These types of arguments are examples of deliberation, not interest-group politics. For an elaboration of the role of deliberation in administrative law, see Shapiro 1988 and Eskridge 1991b.

itics is interest-group politics.[12] In this view, political battles over these arcane details of legislation are common and hard fought, as interest groups and legislators recognize that the structures and procedures specified in the current time period will greatly affect the range of actions and outcomes possible in the future. Because of this realization, actors treat the courts as endogenous and, to an extent, malleable. Normative principles, such as fairness and justice, are undoubtedly important. But interest groups will realize which types of provisions are most likely to help them achieve their goals and will pressure members of Congress to write such provisions into law.

Are such provisions foolproof? Certainly not. First of all, as will be discussed in later chapters, there is a great amount of uncertainty surrounding all of these actions. In addition, at times courts will establish their own rules of procedure, and some of these may be in opposition to what members of Congress would prefer. Specifying review provisions in legislation, however, increases the likelihood that courts will act in certain ways and not in others. And concrete legislative directives present a high hurdle for any court seeking to act in a contrary manner. By specifying certain review provisions, political actors are not looking for a foolproof way of achieving some specific policy objective, but rather are attempting to increase the probability of beneficial outcomes.

Research Questions

Two questions become central at this point. The first question is whether or not actors truly behave this way when creating legislation. Do they attempt to structure judicial review in such a way as to secure political advantage in the future? The second and related question concerns when, and under what conditions, Congress and members of interest groups will seek to expose an agency's decisions to judicial review. At the extreme, if the courts' role is simply that of a guardian to protect against administrative overreaches, we generally would not expect to see interest groups or other members of the enacting coalition lobbying for favorable judicial review provisions. And if such lobbying does occur, we would not expect it to be rooted in self-interest or to be successful. If, on the other hand, interest-group politics reaches this far into procedural details and manages to affect the legislation, then we have support for the alternative proposition. Similarly, we would expect to see that political actors will support provisions that are more likely to enhance the probability that their policy goals will be reached.

---

12. The interest groups and members of Congress can be thought of as members of an "enacting coalition." For a discussion and elaboration of this concept, see McNollgast 1992.

Several other hypotheses emerge from this perspective. Take, for example, the strategic situation faced by an interest group. To the extent that this group feels that the administrative agency is (or will be) sympathetic to its interests, it will be more likely to push for provisions that limit or even preclude judicial review. Similarly, a group that feels it will be disadvantaged by administrative actions will seek to make the bureaucratic process as open to review as possible. In addition, we might expect that local interest groups would prefer to have review centered in local courts, as these courts are likely to be more sympathetic, and less costly, to a local group.

As a group decides which types of provisions to support and promote, however, it does so with the awareness that it cannot easily single itself out for the privileges of judicial review while simultaneously shutting out its opponents. That is, if a group, for whatever reason, favors an easily triggered role for the courts, it must be aware that its opponents also may benefit from such a standard. In other words, the group must consider the overall effects of different review provisions.

This is not to imply that a group will oppose some provision merely because inclusion of the provision may benefit an opposing group. Rather, the group will be careful to look at whether the inclusion of a provision could redound to its detriment if used by an opposing group. In such a case, the benefits a group may accrue from the inclusion of such a provision might be outweighed by the costs of having the provision used against it.

Related Studies

The types of questions addressed by this study are directly analogous to those that have been asked about the relationship between Congress and the bureaucracy. In briefly reviewing this literature, again it is useful to think in terms of a three-stage stylized model of the policy process in which the Congress is the principal and the bureaucracy is the agent. In the final stage, the principal has the opportunity and option to react to the agent's decisions. In the penultimate stage, the agent makes decisions about policy choices. And in the first stage, the principal creates the procedures and structures within which the agents make decisions.

Until recently, studies of this relationship generally focused on the final stage and Congress's willingness and ability to actively oversee the bureaucracy. Most studies concluded that Congress has little incentive to oversee the bureaucracy and, in many cases, has weak control over agencies. A later set of studies challenged this conventional wisdom, however, arguing that subtler mechanisms of control are at work, that in actuality bureaucrats are finely attuned to congressional preferences, and that agencies' outputs reflect these preferences.[13]

Recently, however, a new strain of research has emerged, one that looks at the first stage, or what I earlier referred to as the front end, of the policy-making process. Studies of this type examine how political principals attempt to limit the discretion of agents; how they attempt to reduce (or at least plan for) uncertainty; and how they attempt to do these things a priori.[14] The general thrust of this research is that the second and third stages of the process are not the only chances for the principal to affect the agency's decision; the initial stage also presents such an opportunity.

There are numerous reasons why rational political actors need to take account of the likely consequences of their current choices. One reason is made explicit by McCubbins, Noll, and Weingast (1989) in their examination of the Clean Air Act Amendments of 1977. These authors use a spatial model to demonstrate that once a policy is changed, it may be impossible for the coalition that enacted the original policy to move the policy back to the initial location, even if the preferences of the coalition remain unchanged. This principle is true regardless of whether the change is due to an action taken by the bureaucracy or a decision made by a court. The explanation for this inability to return to the original policy is straightforward—the new policy may be preferred to the original policy by some set of actors, and this set of actors may be able to stop the passage of legislation that would be needed to reenact the original policy.

To counter this possibility, according to these authors, the enacting coalition has an incentive to create structures and procedures that constrain potential future actions undertaken by an agency.[15] The central problem, as they conceive of it, is one of bureaucratic drift. Because of the slack inherent in any principal-agent relationship, agencies may not implement the policy desired by the enacting coalition. To prevent this drift, political actors—Congress, the president, the interested groups—will seek to limit the amount of drift that can take place.

---

13. One of the first attempts to measure such subtle influence was Weingast and Moran 1983. Aberbach (1990) demonstrates that the use of "traditional" oversight has increased dramatically since the 1970s.

14. An interesting, albeit heretofore unacknowledged, parallel exists between this literature and some of Herbert Simon's classic work in organization theory. In particular, the concept that political actors attempt to use procedures and structures to help ensure certain types of outcomes is very similar to Simon's notion that organizational leaders structure the value and factual premises on which other members of the organization make decisions (1957, 45–56).

15. For an extension of this model, see Macey 1992a. On the other hand, criticisms of the concept of the enacting coalition can be found in G. Robinson 1989b; Moe 1990b; and Hill and Brazier 1991.

This problem of bureaucratic drift is, in essence, a form of uncertainty. It reflects the principal's uncertainty about the future course of the agent's actions. That is, once members of Congress delegate policy-making responsibility to an agency, they cannot know with certainty what actions the agency will take. In addition, they are uncertain about which policy issues and questions will arise in the future. As the enacting coalition knows, new and unexpected questions and issues are bound to arise, and while these cannot be known in advance, the coalition can attempt to create structures and procedures that will help the bureaucracy reach an outcome in line with what the current coalition would prefer.

While these types of uncertainty are undoubtedly important, there are other causes of uncertainty that may have as great an effect on the calculations of the original actors. Not only are actors worried about bureaucratic drift and about the unknown decisions that are likely to come up in the future, they also are concerned about the possibility that while they possess political power now, they might not in the future.[16] This concern is central to McCubbins, Noll, and Weingast's concept of "autopilot," which they argue is a way to set an agency's decision making to ensure future policy success and also to protect against the possibility of losing power in the future.

This point is emphasized even more strongly by Moe in a series of articles (1989, 1990a, 1990b), and it, along with the argument that groups must compromise in order to get legislation passed, leads him to reach different conclusions than do McCubbins, Noll, and Weingast.[17] Moe contends that "political uncertainty" is likely to cause actors to favor structures and procedures that they would not favor on technical grounds alone. One result of this uncertainty, he argues, is that actors who are involved in creating agencies may try to place these agencies out of the reach of *all* political actors—themselves included. The reason for such action is the fear that other actors may gain political power and then take control of the agency and use it in a different manner.

Despite the differences in the approaches and conclusions of these studies, their similarities are strong. In particular, they share a common link in emphasizing the strong political incentives to specify procedural

---

16. This type of uncertainty is addressed most explicitly by Moe (1989, 1990a), Horn and Shepsle (1989), and Horn (1995). See also Ferejohn and Weingast's 1992 discussion of how the current Congress, uncertain about the future composition of Congress, attempts to constrain future Congresses.

17. In essence, Moe argues that because legislation is so hard to pass, compromise must take place. That generally means bringing the "opposing group" into the legislative decision-making process, and these other actors will, according to Moe, do whatever they can to cripple the agency. Left unclear, however, is why the winning group would stand for passage of an act that yields a crippled agency.

and structural details in the front end of the policy process. And they explicitly view current choices as a way to structure future decisions and outcomes.

Moving to the Courts

A similar logic can be applied to the courts. What it demonstrates is that political actors arguably have some influence over judicial actions in the second and third stages of the policy process. However, because the ability to influence the courts at these points of the process is limited, the incentives of political actors to design control mechanisms ex ante are heightened.

In the final stage of the policy process, political actors may attempt to overcome court actions—for example, Congress may write a law that overturns a court decision. However, members of Congress will not want to rely on such actions as the only means of dealing with the courts. To begin with, Congress is not always successful in its attempts to overturn court decisions.[18] Part of any lack of success undoubtedly stems from the inherent difficulties involved in passing legislation. For example, even when a majority in Congress prefers to overturn a court decision, this majority may be so hampered by institutional features of Congress that it is unable to achieve its goals (Marks 1988). Another contributing factor is that members of Congress often defer to judicial judgments. This norm of congressional deference to the courts is especially strong for the Judiciary Committee (Miller 1990, 1992). An additional factor is that most members of Congress are often just plain unaware of court decisions, especially if the decision was issued by a lower court (Katzmann 1988, 1992).

One other factor looms large in the decision calculus of political actors. Even if Congress and the president do manage to pass a law in reaction to a court decision, it is likely that the new policy will be different from the status quo ante.[19] There may be a new president, for example, or there may be a different distribution of preferences in Congress, leading to a different policy outcome. To ensure fidelity to their goals, members of the original coalition thus will prefer using constraints on the courts to opening the Pandora's box of new legislation.

How much influence do political actors have over courts in the second

---

18. The most complete and impressive canvassing of congressional reactions to Supreme Court decisions can be found in an article by William Eskridge (1991b). In this article, Eskridge reports that since 1967, Congress has overturned an average of five Supreme Court statutory-interpretation decisions per year. For statistical evaluations of such override attempts, see Ignagni and Meernik 1994 and Bawn and Shipan 1993.

19. On this point, again see McCubbins, Noll and Weingast 1989.

stage of the policy process? Again, that is difficult to ascertain, but to the extent that judges are political actors with policy preferences, they wish to see their most preferred policies implemented. To achieve these outcomes they must take into account the policy preferences of other actors (e.g., Spiller and Gely 1992; Ferejohn and Shipan 1988, 1990; Eskridge 1991a).

Strategic behavior by judges undoubtedly occurs.[20] However, courts frequently will have a wide range of outcomes to choose from, and there is no assurance that the outcome they select will be one favored by Congress or the president. The relative weakness of sanctions means that compliance is much less likely in the case of the courts than in the case of agencies. While there are certain powers members of Congress and presidents hold over courts, these powers are difficult to use, often very blunt, may appear illegitimate, and are almost never employed.[21] Although judges are influenced by the perceived preferences of other political actors, this influence is unquestionably less common and more idiosyncratic than in the case of agencies. And it is almost certainly even less true for lower courts than for the Supreme Court.

The uncertainty of power over courts in the second and third stages of the policy process leaves political actors with an even stronger incentive to pay close attention to procedural details during the front end of the policy process. All outcomes undeniably are not determined at this stage by actors who have perfect information and infallible foresight, but interest groups, legislators, and the president all have an incentive to try to constrain future actions, especially because such actions may be difficult to overturn in the future. That is even truer for courts than for agencies. While there are ready avenues for addressing bureaucratic "missteps" and for putting pressure on bureaucrats as they make decisions, fewer such options are available in the case of the courts. This lack of options heightens the incentives of other actors to anticipate and plan, ex ante, for court action.

---

20. See Murphy 1964. The extent to which such behavior occurs, however, is somewhat controversial and is currently under investigation. L. Epstein and Knight (1995) provide evidence of strategic interaction between justices and Smith and Tiller (1996) argue that judges act strategically in choosing judicial instruments; however, Segal (1995) finds little evidence of strategic behavior with respect to other political actors. Segal contends that the lack of strategic behavior is the central difference between two overtly political theories of courts—the positive models discussed here and the attitudinal model summarized in Segal and Spaeth 1993.

21. While Congress is not impotent with respect to the courts, its powers are somewhat limited, especially in comparison to its powers over the bureaucracy. Posner summarizes these limited powers as follows: "Congress can refuse to raise judges' salaries in times of inflation, can curtail their perquisites, can be stingy in appropriating money for essential support services, can impose onerous duties on the judges with one hand and curtail their jurisdiction with the other, can overrule non-constitutional decisions, can initiate constitutional amendments, can add new judges and new courts, and in these and other ways can show effective displeasure with the judges" (1985, 21).

Although writers of legislation do not have perfect information about the effects of the judicial review provisions they choose, they take whatever information they have into account when writing judicial review provisions into regulatory (and other) statutes. Furthermore, one can argue that these initial provisions greatly affect the actual policy outcomes (e.g., Cass 1989). This study lends support to this view and in so doing gives us a new way to think about the role of the courts in the political process.

The Analysis

To check for influence by interest groups and members of Congress on the creation of judicial review provisions, I focus on the origins of broadcast regulation, and in particular on the passage of the Communications Act of 1934. While arguments could be made for focusing on more than one policy area, an in-depth study of one area is appropriate and valuable. In analyses of this type it often is difficult to tell which procedural provisions are necessitated by features endemic to the policy and which are actually instances of political maneuvering and attempts to exert control. Concentrating on one policy area helps alleviate this hazard. Furthermore, focusing on one area will allow me to investigate several aspects of the causes and effects of judicial review, as I will detail in later chapters.

The Communications Act is a particularly interesting target for several reasons. To begin with, communications policy is an area in which the courts have played an active and prominent role.[22] In addition, this law was passed before the era of congressional micromanagement of agency policy-making. As opposed to some of the social regulatory acts of the 1960s and 1970s, which ran into the hundreds of pages, the entire Communications Act is less than fifty pages long. Any findings of battles over review provisions in such a case are therefore even more resonant. Furthermore, because it was enacted during an era in which administrative and regulatory agencies were first being considered and used on a large scale, it provides an especially fertile area in which to examine judicial review.[23]

Finally, there is the nature of the creation of the Federal Communications Commission (FCC). The main effect of the Communications Act was to bring together regulation of common carriers such as telephones and railroads, which until that time had fallen under the jurisdiction of the Interstate Commerce Commission (ICC), and regulation of broadcasting,

---

22. See, for example, Ginsburg 1979, Jameson 1979, Ulloth 1979, and examples throughout Cass and Diver 1987.

23. Jaffe, for example, has remarked, "Until the era of modern social legislation, it was not usually considered necessary to make specific provision for judicial control of administration action" (1965, 158).

which at the time was controlled by the Federal Radio Commission (FRC) under the Federal Radio Act of 1927. The Communications Act of 1934 therefore can be considered a manifestation of the tendency during the New Deal era to centralize administrative activities. Surprisingly, however, even though two very different and distinctive industries were being brought together under one regulatory roof, there was almost no controversy over whether this consolidation was appropriate (G. Robinson 1989a). Controversy did arise, however, over the nature of judicial review to which the industries would be subjected. In fact, many observers at the time saw this as one of the primary issues of contention during the debates leading up to the passage of the Communications Act. A typical contemporary observation can be found in a note in the *Virginia Law Review,* which contended that "the greatest difficulty which confronted the framers of the Act was that of appeals from decisions and rulings of the Commission" (Note 1934, 323).[24]

During the debates over the act, several different controversies arose about judicial review. Some disputes dealt with the specific provisions that detailed the extent to which agency decisions would be reviewable.[25] In particular, controversy arose over whether the broadcasting industry should be subjected to the type of review that had been applied to the actions of the FRC or to the more limited type of review that had been applied to the decisions of the ICC.[26] Additionally, there was a great deal of discussion over which court would be given review powers. Hence, this act represents a paradigmatic example of the importance of judicial review.

These and other ideas and controversies are explored more fully in the next two chapters, in which I focus on the theoretical aspects of judicial review. Following these theoretical chapters, I relate the history and describe the nature of communications policy in the 1920s and 1930s, with a special emphasis on the nature and structure of the broadcasting industry. In light of this background discussion and the general theory, I then examine the goals and actions of members of the enacting coalition. Included in this analysis are discussions of which interest groups were

---

24. Similarly, see Berman 1933 and Seidman 1934, as well as various issues of the trade journal *NAB Reports,* for additional contemporary discussions of the centrality of the review provisions to participants.

25. The specifics of these battles are presented in chapters 5 and 6.

26. As will be detailed later, there were two primary differences between provisions for review of ICC and FRC actions. First, ICC decisions were appealable only to district courts, whereas FRC decisions could also be appealed to the Court of Appeals for the District of Columbia. Second, it was unclear whether the ICC provisions, if applied to radio stations, would have allowed for the appeal of "negative orders" made by the commission, where such negative orders would have included the revocation or denial of licenses.

involved, what their incentives were, and what actions they took regarding the inclusion of judicial review provisions. I then take these preferences into account and examine the incentives faced by Congress and the action taken by Congress. Finally, in the concluding chapter I discuss the general applicability of the theoretical perspective and suggest future avenues for study.

CHAPTER 2

Interest Groups, Congress, and Preferences over Judicial Review Provisions

When political actors attempt to influence court decisions through the judicious selection of review provisions, how do they decide which provisions will be most advantageous? In this chapter I begin to address this question by engaging in a theoretical exploration of the political and strategic aspects of designing judicial review provisions. Looking first at interest groups and then at Congress, I investigate the goals of political actors with respect to judicial review, the tools that are available to these actors, and the sources of information that these actors use to determine which review provisions will be most beneficial. This exploration will be used as a building block for chapter 3, wherein I develop a more general theory of review.

Four overlapping claims will be advanced. First, judicial review provisions, far from being purely technical or legal details, are also political variables. Second, groups and members of Congress recognize the importance of institutional design and therefore pay attention to the likely consequences of their institutional choices. Third, interest groups may at times push for provisions that might appear to be less than optimal, in part because of the calculated effect of these provisions on other groups. Finally, the stylized policy process implicit in the traditional model, in which judicial review becomes important only after an agency has acted, is flawed. Instead, actors in the early stages of the policy process consider what is likely to be done in later stages by the courts, and they try to take these potential judicial actions into consideration when writing legislation.

In addition to emphasizing interest groups' and legislators' use of judicial review provisions to channel and constrain the actions of courts, another concept will be stressed: the role played by information, which is key in three ways. First, as mentioned before, political actors use different sources of information to help them choose provisions. Second, the *amount* of information affects the types of provisions these actors will choose. And third, these actors use procedures to try to control the exposure of the courts to various kinds of information.

Interest Groups and Procedural "Details"

Most constituents do not consider the political battles over procedural details to be important. As a result, most constituents pay little, if any, attention to these battles. However, for specific groups of constituents—namely, interest groups—these battles are of central consequence. Because of the intensity of their interest, such groups find it worthwhile to invest resources in determining which procedures and structures are likely to be most beneficial. They understand that procedures and structures specified in legislation are not neutral, that some procedures and structures are more likely to result in favorable outcomes than are others. While normative principles such as fairness and justice undoubtedly influence choices, structures and procedures are some of the tools by which interest groups can attempt to gain political advantage.[1] And because of the significance of these details interest groups do pay a great deal of attention to them.[2] It is for this reason that I begin this analysis of judicial review by looking at interest groups.[3]

Why would interest groups worry about a detail like judicial review provisions? To begin with, a group will know that procedural and structural constraints on an agency are imperfect means of control, as are ex post sanctions designed to correct bureaucratic actions with which the group (or Congress) disagrees. While carefully designed bureaucratic

---

1. While most analysts would agree that structures affect outcomes (e.g., Polenberg 1966; Wilson 1985, 1990; Moe 1989; Macey 1992a, 1992b), see G. Robinson 1989b for the unusual argument that the structure or location of an agency makes little difference. For another critical view of the importance of structure and procedure, see Hill and Brazier 1991. On the importance of normative principles, see West 1985 and McNollgast 1992.

2. Interest groups thus can be regarded as *consequentialist*. That is, they know that their actions will have consequences and they attempt to act in ways that produce their most-preferred consequences. For an elaboration of the contrary view that political actors attempt to choose the most *appropriate* action rather than the one with the most favorable consequences, see March and Olsen 1989.

3. It is important, however, not to fall into the trap of regarding interest-group preferences as completely deterministic. An interesting example of a group losing a major battle over an agency's structure occurred in the field of radio regulation during the 1920s. For several years, the radio industry pushed hard to procure federal regulation to control the incipient chaos in the broadcasting industry. Radio interests were virtually unanimous in their opinion that regulation under the auspices of the Department of Commerce was preferable to regulation by a new independent commission, and they were joined in this opinion by officials of the executive branch. Nonetheless, in the 1927 Radio Act, Congress created an independent commission to regulate radio.

structures and administrative arrangements can influence agency decisions to a large extent, control remains far from perfect. The group knows that even if an agency, induced in part by structural provisions, is somewhat likely to make favorable decisions, some decisions will be contrary to the group's desires, and it may want the opportunity to appeal these decisions to the courts. In such cases, the group views judicial action as a "second chance" to achieve an agreeable outcome. On the other hand, if the agency seems highly likely to make favorable decisions, the group may prefer to keep the courts out of the process. The agency may indeed act in ways favorable to the group. In this case, the group would prefer that the courts *not* interfere in the policy arena, that instead the process should end with the favorable agency decision.

Thus, based on uncertainty about agency actions, in some instances groups may want the courts to get involved, while in others they may want the courts to remain out of the picture. But a new problem then arises: there is likely to be uncertainty over court actions, too. The problem, then, becomes how to account for and constrain the courts. As discussed in the first chapter, ex post mechanisms that can be used to influence bureaucracies are much weaker or do not even exist with respect to the courts. Furthermore, lifetime tenure gives judges a measure of freedom that bureaucrats do not have. Because of the weakness of sanctions and controls over the courts, an interest group pushing for specific legislation has an added incentive to consider what the courts may do. The puzzle for the group is how to make the best use of the courts.

The importance of the courts to interest groups has not gone unnoticed, of course. Many of the classic works on pluralism, for example, have acknowledged the importance of the courts to interest groups.[4] But while several scholars have analyzed interest group strategies vis-à-vis the courts, their focus generally has been on tactics used during or leading up to court cases.[5] In particular, scholars have centered their attention on a few strategies used by the groups, such as the sponsoring of test cases and class action suits, the filing of amicus curiae briefs, the influencing of appointments, and even the shaping of opinion in the legal community (L. Epstein 1991; Schlozman and Tierney 1986). Yet, as

---

4. See, for example, the strong statement by Truman (1951, 479–80). Other classic works of pluralism, such as Bentley 1908 and Latham 1952, also include discussions of interest-group attention to the judiciary. Yet despite the obvious importance of the courts to interest groups and cases like *Webster v. Reproductive Health Services* (192 U.S. 190 [1989]), where more than four hundred groups participated, only recently have scholars zeroed in on the relationship between interest groups and courts (L. Epstein 1991).

5. This is a large literature, including work by Caldiera and Wright (1988), L. Epstein (1985), O'Connor (1980), Sorauf (1976), Tushnet (1987), and Vose (1959).

Epstein acknowledges in her thoughtful review of the literature on courts and interest groups, "Much work remains, though, before we have a fully developed picture of this aspect of group litigation. For one thing, have we tapped all the strategies groups use to influence the judiciary?" (1991, 349).

One such strategy, heretofore unexamined, is the writing into law of specific provisions for judicial review. As noted in the previous chapter, there is an analogue here to the use of structure and process to shape bureaucratic actions. In the first stage of the policy process—the front end of the policy process—interest groups can try to structure the decisions courts will make at a later stage. They can do so not by proscribing outcomes in certain cases (which, given lack of knowledge and imperfect information, would present almost insuperable obstacles), but rather by constraining what actions are and are not permissible for the courts to undertake. Judicial review provisions provide groups with an opportunity to think about which decisions, on which grounds, by which groups, and in which courts, will be reviewed.

All interest groups will have an incentive to affect the design of such provisions. For example, Moe notes that a group possessing political power will "favor making various types of agency actions—or inactions—appealable to the courts. It must take care to design these procedures and checks, however, so that they disproportionately favor the groups over its opponents" (1989, 275). On the other hand, Moe also allows that opposition groups may have a similar incentive to structure judicial review provisions. He argues that they "will favor an active, easily triggered role for the courts in reviewing agency decisions" (1989, 276). Moe is undoubtedly correct that interest groups have an incentive to anticipate court action. What we need to think about is *how* they will do so.

The Tools

The most direct way groups can plan ahead for court involvement is by influencing the way in which courts decide cases.[6] While most debates over the role of the judiciary take place in the language of concepts like fairness and due process, _the exact nature of judicial review of administrative action is also a political variable_. Although many studies of judicial review simply take the nature and status of review as a given and then proceed to a normative discussion, or else assume that courts unilaterally set the terms of review, the terms of review are not a "given" but rather are malleable and

---

6. An indirect way they can do so is by influencing elections, thereby attempting to influence what kinds of judges get appointed to the courts.

manipulable. Because of this malleability, groups will seek to influence the design of judicial review.

There are two main ways interest groups can influence review of agency actions. First, they can take aim at statutory interpretation. A carefully placed phrase in the legislative history or committee reports, a stealthy insertion into the congressional record, use of postenactment cues or presidential signing statements—all of these can be used to influence future statutory review, as many judges rely on such sources in their attempts to discern congressional intent.[7]

The relevance of such actions is captured by Melnick (1994) in his incisive examination of welfare legislation. In his case studies, he observed that members of Congress, spurred by interest groups, paid close attention to the potential effects of their statements and actions on future statutory interpretations. Even when members were motivated by genuine public-interest concerns, they still thought strategically about how current legislative actions might play out in the arena of the courts in the future.

While these kinds of actions can influence judicial review, the focus of this study is on how groups can influence the availability, type, and costs of review by strategically choosing specific provisions for judicial review. There are several ways in which they can do so. For example, consider the placement of the *burden of proof,* a so-called detail that fueled a large portion of the debate in the early 1990s over revisions to civil rights law. An interest group seeking political advantage will attempt to place the burden of proof on its opponents (which may include the government, if the government is trying impose restrictions on the industry). Accordingly, businesses wanted employees to have to demonstrate the existence of discrimination and opposed legislation that put the onus on them to demonstrate that no discrimination had occurred. Employees, on the other hand, wanted employers to have to demonstrate the absence of discrimination. As the burden of proof can be quite heavy, each side sought to have the weight placed on its opponents.

The burden of proof is just one of several provisions that can be specified and are the subject of political calculation. In this study I also focus on four other types of provisions that are commonly fought over. First, groups may seek to obtain *standing* for themselves or to deny it to their opponents. Second, in order to specify to the courts the grounds on

7. Heclo observes: "Suppose you are a new member of Congress. . . . You are now one of the many scattered targets of opportunity for interest groups to pursue their causes and influence executive agency actions. The courts may be more willing to take action on issues of importance to your agenda; if not, interest groups and staff will help your subcommittee write language in legislation and reports that will encourage them to do so" (1989, 316). See also Melnick 1985 on the "partnership" between judges and agencies.

which judicial decisions may be made, they may seek either a restrictive or an expansive *scope of review*. Third, they may wish to stipulate in the legislation the terms of *reviewability*. For example, legislation may indicate that certain agency decisions are not reviewable by the courts or that other decisions specifically are reviewable. And finally, groups may seek to have review vested in a *specific court* (or courts), perhaps for reasons of cost or perhaps because one court has a reputation for being more sympathetic to their cause.[8]

What does the group hope to gain through the careful specification of such procedures? As discussed earlier, the group knows that in many cases it will want the courts to step in and review an agency's decision. However, it will not want to provide the judiciary with carte blanche power, as that could put the group in a situation where it actually might be made worse off than with no review. The group instead will use provisions such as those mentioned in the previous paragraph to affect judicial outcomes.

Again, an analogy exists. When Congress, with the approval of certain groups, delegates responsibility to an agency, it does not give unconditional authority to that agency. Instead, it carefully designs the agency to minimize the potential for bureaucratic drift (McCubbins, Noll, and Weingast 1987). In other words, political actors carefully design bureaucratic procedures with the intent of channeling agency actions toward preferred outcomes.

As they do with bureaucratic provisions, political actors will choose judicial review provisions that will help them receive favorable outcomes in the future. There are two ways in which this is done. First, groups will push for legislation that specifies, in some instances, *how* the court is to act. A provision designating the terms of reviewability, for example, tells the courts which agency actions can be reviewed and which cannot. Specifying which courts are eligible to hear appeals similarly limits the actions of groups. Such provisions affect how the judiciary goes about making its decisions, much as bureaucratic structures and procedures affect how agencies reach their decisions.

Of equal importance in designing these provisions is the role of *information*. Information is key is three ways. First, as will be discussed in the next section, groups use different sources of information in trying to determine what types of provisions to push for.

---

8. Other considerations include whether a special court was created, such as the Commerce Court created in 1910 by the Mann-Elkins Act; whether there is an explicit standard of review (as opposed to "arbitrary and capricious" or "unsupported by evidence"); details about exhaustion; the awarding of attorneys' fees; specification of the statute of limitations; and severability. Several of these factors are explored by Shapiro (1968), who notes that such rules defining judicial review are largely made by the courts.

Second, the *amount* of information and knowledge about a policy area plays an important role. As mentioned before, if a group possessed the ability to foresee all future developments, it could design legislation that deals with the most minute details of policy. Since we live in a world of uncertainty, however, groups and legislators instead must use whatever information they have about a policy area when designing procedures. And if there is a low level of information about a policy area, or a great deal of uncertainty surrounding the potential developments in an area, the groups will not want to write detailed provisions that might hinder the development of their field. In such cases, the amount of information about future developments is important because it determines the amount of flexibility the group needs to build into both the agency and the judicial procedures.

The final way in which information plays a role is especially relevant at this point. The careful use of procedures can direct the courts to act in certain ways. Again, however, there will be many circumstances that are unforeseen and for which specific procedures cannot be written. What interest groups need to do, then, is control the *type* of information that the courts receive. In other words, groups will push for provisions that limit the types of information to which the courts are exposed.

Obviously, legislation rarely tells the courts to listen to one side of an argument but not the other. Provisions can be used, however, to control the *access* of different groups to the courts and, in so doing, can determine which points of view the courts will hear. While several types of provisions affect the courts' access to information, by far the most important is the specification of standing. For if a group is guaranteed standing, its point of view will at a minimum be heard by the judiciary, whereas if a group is denied standing, it loses assurance that the courts will be exposed to its point of view.[9]

The Group's Calculations

As should be apparent, an interest group has to choose from a large variety of options during the front end of the policy process. Choosing among alternatives for the structures and procedures of an agency presents one set of hurdles; thinking about the courts adds yet another layer of complexity to the group's consequentialist determinations.

What considerations will affect a group's actions? In general, the group will want to contemplate what types of biases the courts might have.

---

9. On this point, see Rabin's 1986 discussion of environmental interest groups in the 1960s.

It needs to consider whether the courts are generally sympathetic to its cause. A business interest group, for example, will consider whether the courts are generally probusiness or prolabor, proregulation or antiregulation. More specifically, since there is not one "court" but rather many courts, the group will examine *which* courts are likely to favor them and which are not. Furthermore, the group will want to determine whether there is a difference between judicial levels. That is, are courts more likely to be sympathetic at the state or federal level (if that is a viable choice)? Will district courts be more sympathetic than courts of appeals?[10]

Finally, groups also need to consider carefully what effects different provisions will have on their opponents. This does not mean that a group will decide whether to support or oppose a provision or set of provisions based simply on the expectation of a provision's impact on its opponents. What it *does* mean is that a group may oppose a provision, even one that might seem beneficial, if the expected utility of the provision is negative (i.e., if it is likely to benefit their opponents and eventually hurt them).

This point is key. Many provisions, once enacted, will be available to anyone. A group therefore may make what seems like a peculiar choice simply because it is sophisticated enough not to look at the effect of a provision in isolation—that is, the effect only on itself. Instead, a group needs to consider the overall effect of a provision. Because judicial review is often a two-way street, groups must acknowledge that not only will they be able to take advantage of a provision, but other groups may be able to use the provisions against them.

The same is, of course, true with most procedures. Consider, for example, a regulated industry that wants easy access to the courts. It may push for provisions that enhance its ability to sue an agency. Because the agency does not want to be sued, it will become finely attuned to the desires of the group. The group's strategy may backfire, however, because an opposing group also may be able to take advantage of the opportunity to sue the agency. Therefore, the group must think hard about what types of provisions to favor.

Underlying much of this calculation is the simple idea that groups must know who their opponents are. On the one hand, this idea is relatively obvious—business, for example, generally knows that labor will oppose many of the things it wants. On the other hand, groups also must be cognizant of latent, or potential, interest groups—people with a shared interest who have not yet formed into a group but nonetheless represent a potential opponent (Truman 1951; Olson 1965).

---

10. Glick (1988) and Richardson and Vines (1970) enumerate several reasons why district courts may be biased toward local interests, noting in particular that no district courts cross state lines and that federal judges must live in the districts in which they serve.

TABLE 2.1.   Factors Affecting Preferences over Judicial Review Provisions

Experience	with the courts and, in some cases, the agency
Legal regime	includes the general relationship between courts and agencies and the role of general court doctrine
Institutional theories	perceptions of each institution's capabilities
Other interest groups	recognition of who the other groups are, and of the costs and benefits of judicial review to these other groups

Given the panoply of options available, and given that actors have preferences over outcomes and ergo over the structures and procedures that will shape those outcomes, how do actors choose among alternatives? Formally, if j_i are judicial review provisions, then a group will prefer j_1 to j_2 if $EU(j_1) > EU(j_2)$. Further, let v_a be the value of an expected agency decision, v_j be the value of an expected court decision, and p be the probability that the court overturns the agency decision.[11] The expected utility is a function of these three variables, as follows:

$$EU(j_i) = p(j_i)v_j(j_i) + (1 - p(j_i))v_a$$

For the interest group to calculate the expected utility of each provision, it needs to come up with a value for each of the different parameters. One way it does so is by considering the factors mentioned earlier, such as the effects of the provisions on opposing groups.

Of course, to determine net benefits, the group also will need to determine the likely effect of each provision. My argument is that interest groups will rely on past experience, current legal trends, and theories of the courts and bureaucracies to help them sort out all of these different possibilities (see table 2.1). By using these various sources of information, judicial action, while not completely endogenous, can be considered and partially accounted for in the first stage of the policy process. The implication is that while courts are not completely controllable, they are constrainable.

In the following sections I will discuss the sources of information a group can use to assign values to these parameters—experience, general information about prevailing court-agency relations, and an institutional approach. While these sources are not mutually exclusive, I will first dis-

---

11. Both p and v_j are functions of j. That is, both the probability of the court overturning the agency decision and the expected nature of the judicial decision depend on the nature of the judicial review provision.

cuss them in isolation from each other to make clear the basic outline of each approach, proceeding from the least abstract (experiential) to the most abstract (institutional).

Experience

Experiential information comes from the interest group's *prior substantive experience* with the courts and agencies. Decisions within these units tend to show a fair degree of stability over time, and concerned interest groups, more than any other constituents, will be aware of this consistency.

This source of information is most useful when existing regulatory legislation is being amended. If a policy has been in effect for several years, and an agency and court have been making decisions about this policy, an interest group will have a good sense of the likely biases of agencies and courts. Then, when legislation is being rewritten, the group will examine its past experience with the courts and agencies and from this examination will try to predict what they will do in the future. The group then will act accordingly to structure judicial review.

How will the group evaluate the situation in such cases? It will look at how favorable or unfavorable the actions of both the agency and the courts have been. Some of the outcomes are easy to predict—when court decisions have been favorable but the agency has been less friendly, for example, the interest group will favor a lenient set of review provisions. The members of groups will view the courts as yet another tool through which they can attempt to control—or at least constrain—the agency, and they therefore will give the courts wide latitude in reviewing the agency's decisions.

Similarly, given a friendly agency and an unfriendly judiciary, the interest group will want to shield the actions of the agency from judicial review.[12] To that end, it will want judicial review to be difficult to trigger, with the goal of constraining the courts as much as possible. By doing so, it hopes to give the agency the last word on policy decisions. While this constraint does not shut out the courts, it makes it much more difficult for them to act, as they will have to find a controversy of a constitutional (rather than statutory) nature.[13]

Finally, what about the other two possibilities—first, both the agency

---

12. This situation is elucidated and illustrated by the spatial model in chapter 3.

13. And, as many scholars have observed, courts generally prefer, if possible, to rule on statutory rather than on constitutional grounds. That courts can rule on constitutional grounds if they so choose indicates a limitation of the effects of review provisions. I might also note that courts generally agreed with the constitutionality of the statutory prohibition against judicial review of Veterans Administration benefit decisions (discussed in chapter 7).

and the court are considered friendly, and second, both are considered unfriendly? These situations cannot be classified as cleanly as the others, and if these situations exist, it is likely that the two information sources yet to be discussed will gain in importance. However, the interest group still will attempt to determine which institution is more likely to be friendly, now and in the future, and it will favor legislation that gives that actor the final move in the policy process.[14]

Legal Regime

The legal regime is more abstract than the aforementioned experiential approach and consequently covers a wider range of cases. Yet while more general, it also can provide more insight into why specific provisions of judicial review are chosen. It also can help determine whether interest groups even want the courts to be involved.

This approach, as suggested by its name, puts a great deal of emphasis on prevailing views about the legal and administrative system as an explanatory variable.[15] The legal regime plays a role in at least two very important respects. First, it defines what types of provisions are at issue; in other words, it defines the feasible set of provisions over which debate is likely. And second, it defines the general nature of interinstitutional interactions. Let us tackle the second of these first.

Martin Shapiro (1982, 1988) has argued persuasively that administrative law doctrine tends to be a time-lagged version of the previous era's dominant political philosophy. That is, today's administrative law takes its theoretical underpinnings from yesterday's political philosophy. As an example, in the 1950s the group theory of politics, or pluralism, was the predominant mode of both normative and positive studies of the policy process. Yet it was not until the 1960s and early 1970s that the courts assertively sought to ensure that agencies were hearing from a wide array of groups. In other words, the courts started bringing pluralism to agency decision making, but only ten or fifteen years after pluralism first had become the dominant political philosophy.

What can Shapiro's argument tell us about preferences for judicial review provisions? The main point is that there tends to be, in each era, a

---

14. It is worth emphasizing at this point that groups have preferences over *outcomes*. As will be explicated more conclusively later, their preferences over institutions are induced from their expectations about these outcomes.

15. For related analyses of this concept, see Shipan's 1992 and forthcoming (1997) descriptions of the "legal climate" and Eskridge and Ferejohn's 1994 use of "interpretive regimes." Future treatments of this concept may benefit from recognizing that constitutional and statutory review are influenced by different doctrinal developments.

dominant mode of administrative law philosophy. While I would not claim that interest groups slyly read the previous era's classic political theory texts, hoping to gain an advantage once this theory changes lanes and becomes administrative law doctrine, I do contend that groups certainly are aware of the dominant trends in administrative law when they are attempting to determine the expected value of different provisions.

By this logic, interest groups in the 1950s could be relatively certain that judges, who were not technical experts, would defer to agencies, which were. The courts generally would work from the presumptions that the agency, first, had properly found the facts, and second, had correctly interpreted the law. In effect, as Shapiro (1982) trenchantly observes, it was an era characterized by judicial surrender to executive branch lawmaking.

While having an understanding of the basic approach taken by administrative law certainly does not predict a single outcome for each case, that by no means implies that knowledge of such underpinnings is devoid of value for interest groups. Indeed, such an understanding unveils a great deal of information when a group is trying to decide how and when court involvement should be invoked and how and when it should be restrained. Knowing that courts are apt to defer to agency expertise is likely to guide an interest group to prefer one set of provisions, while knowing that the courts are placing heavy demands on agencies (e.g., in the 1970s prior to the *Vermont Yankee* case) will cause it to prefer a different set of provisions.

So far, this discussion of the legal regime has stressed the importance of the general trends in court-agency relations at a given point in time. However, as mentioned earlier, this approach also yields insight into which specific types of provisions are likely to be debated. Let us see how that is so.

Since interest groups have limited resources—time, money, access—which they can use to sway members of Congress, they will try not to waste any of these valuable resources fighting battles that need not be fought.[16] Since judicial review is only a small part of any legislative design, interest groups will be especially careful to focus on only the most important of the many issues that arise in debates over judicial review provisions.

Groups need some way to whittle down the long list of concerns discussed earlier. It is more efficient for them to focus on the most important of the judicial review provisions. But it also makes little sense for them to fight about issues that are not controversial. For example, if it is generally acknowledged that the courts of a given era have a very lenient standard

---

16. For a similar theme, see Austen-Smith and Wright 1994.

for, say, standing, then it makes little sense for the interest group to spend a lot of time and effort putting that into writing. This is not to say that these issues are unimportant; in fact, quite the opposite may be true. The germane point here is that there are certain defaults that exist in the administrative law realm, certain de facto standards of which the interest groups can be relatively certain. Given the limited resources of interest groups, perhaps it is sensible for them to ignore provisions that are relatively settled so they can focus on more uncertain provisions. It would be extremely difficult, costly, and not very fruitful for interest groups to buck the general trend (e.g., to push for a very broad scope of review in the 1950s).

Discerning the Legal Regime   There are several ways in which groups and members of Congress become aware of the legal regime. One way, mentioned earlier, is through observation of the general approach that courts take toward agencies and administrative decisions. Political actors undoubtedly will be aware of trends of the period, such as whether the era is one of judicial deference to the bureaucracy. Another indicator of the legal regime can be found in the general attitudes of political actors, such as members of Congress, toward either courts or agencies. This indicator will be examined later in this chapter.

Specific landmark court cases also may provide a good sign of the legal regime. For example, perhaps the most important set of cases concerning the development of economic regulation in the late 1800s and early 1900s were those indicating the attitude of the judiciary toward property rights. In the late 1800s, the Supreme Court came to reflect the growing national consensus that the path to economic well-being resided in the philosophy of laissez-faire. Previously, the Court had found the basis for this philosophy in the doctrine of vested rights or the idea of natural law.[17] But in the aftermath of the Civil War and the passage of the Fourteenth Amendment, the Court located the basis for protection of property rights in the due process clause. As Justice Robert H. Jackson observed:

> Beginning about 1890, it was a fortunate and relatively innocuous piece of reform legislation that was able to run the gantlet of the due process clause. Two hundred and twenty-eight times thereafter the Supreme Court set aside state legislative action under the Fourteenth Amendment. The figures do not tell the whole story, because a single

---

17. The doctrine of vested rights "is sufficiently described as a notification by the courts that they would disallow any legislative act which they found to bear unduly harshly upon existing property rights. . . ." (Corwin 1934, 56).

decision may have caused the death of similar legislation in many states and prevented its birth in others. (1941, 50)[18]

This adherence to protection of property rights continued into the first decades of the twentieth century. Two defining cases were *Lochner v. New York* and *Hammer v. Dagenhart*.[19] In *Lochner,* a New York statute limiting bakers to a sixty-hour workweek was struck down. In the next decade, this decision was echoed by *Hammer,* in which a federal child labor statute, prohibiting interstate commerce of products made by children, was struck down.

These cases were *not* general indications that the Supreme Court was opposed to any federal intervention in the economy. Far from it.[20] But these cases, and others in the early decades of the twentieth century, do show that the Court was diligent in its protection of private property rights and harbored a strong tendency to critically review regulatory legislation and the actions of regulatory agencies. This hypercriticism was especially evident with respect to newly created agencies (Rabin 1986, 1233).

Such, then, was the atmosphere at the time of the creation of the Federal Radio Commission in 1927. Yet by the time of the creation of the Federal Communications Commission seven years later, the situation was more muddled. One chronicler of the changes in the Supreme Court over this period characterizes the years 1933 and 1934 as a time when the Court hesitated between two worlds, one in which the Court saw itself as a bulwark against excessive government intervention in the economy, the other in which the Court eventually would acquiesce with the initiatives of the New Deal (Jackson 1941).

In the 1934 case of *Nebbia v. New York,* for example, by a vote of five

---

18. Jackson holds up the case of *United States v. E. C. Knight Co.* (156 U.S. 1, 17) as a prototypical example of how far the Supreme Court would go to oppose government regulation and emasculate the Sherman Antitrust Law. In this case, despite control of some 98 percent of the sugar refining business in the United States by the company in question, the Court declared that its activities were manufacturing and not commerce, and thus "could not constitutionally be reached by Congress" (Jackson 1941, 57).

19. The former case was 198 U.S. 45 (1906); the latter, 247 U.S. 251 (1918). For further details on each of these cases and their relationship to broader political currents of the time, see Rabin 1986.

20. Rabin (1986) nicely details the extent to which the Supreme Court *did* allow governmental control of the economy. Even a critic of that Court admits as much: "[The Court] approved or disapproved each law, grudgingly giving consent to any departure from laissez faire, or to any serious interference with the power of property and employers. I do not mean to say that it never did give consent. The Federal Government was confirmed in important powers over railroads, grain and cattle dealings, and many kindred subjects. Workmen's compensation, factory standards, and maximum hours of labor finally became established, though in some cases only after years of judicial obstruction" (Jackson 1941, 70).

to four the Court allowed a state milk board to establish minimum prices designed to eliminate destructive competition.[21] And later that year the Court recognized that sometimes existing conditions justified governmental incursions into the realm of private contracts.[22] While both of these cases were decided by only a single vote, they did signal the possibility that the Supreme Court was moving in a new direction. And while movement in this direction did not last long—the next year the Court turned course and invalidated some New Deal legislation—it is clear that this period was no longer one in which groups could be so certain of the stringent defense of property rights by the Court.

Institutional

Finally, let us turn to the institutional approach. As in the previous approaches, the interest group examines the selection of different review provisions in light of expectations about both the bureaucracy and the courts. Yet whereas the experiential approach was based on past interactions with these other governmental actors, and the legal-regime approach was conditioned by the specific circumstances existing in the era during which the decision is made, the institutional approach reflects an evaluation of the general institutional characteristics of the bureaucracy and the courts. By relying, perhaps implicitly, on general theoretical models of agency and court behavior, the interest group attempts to predict which types of provisions are likely to be in its favor. The general notion is that in order to construct a theory of judicial review, one must first have in mind a theory of bureaucratic and court action.

What are the different theories of bureaucracy that the interest group might rely on? Several candidates exist—bureaucracies as neutral, problem-solving experts; the "transmission belt" theory of bureaucracy; and the notion that bureaucrats are unconstrained actors. Along similar lines, one might conceive of the bureaucracy as the agent of other political actors (Congress, the president, interest groups), and look at the degree to which an agency is constrained by its environment (e.g., the transmission belt theory corresponds to completely constrained agents).[23]

Several theories of courts also have been developed over the years.[24]

---

21. 291 U.S. 502 (1934). As Rabin demonstrates, the Court could have relied on the Munn standard of "businesses affected with a public interest" to reject this price regulation on grounds of substantive due process (1986, 1254).

22. *Home Building and Loan Association v. Blaisdell,* 190 U.S. 398 (1934).

23. On different conceptions of the bureaucratic process, see Stewart 1975.

24. The single best discussion I have seen of various schools of legal thought can be found in Fisher 1991. See also Mensch 1990 and Note 1982.

For example, one characterization of legal realism treats courts as political actors who have their own policy preferences and try to achieve outcomes closest to their ideal points.[25] On the other hand, a traditional legal approach would argue that courts are protectors of rights and due process and therefore have motivations different from those of other political actors.[26]

The specific provisions preferred by interest groups will consequently depend on which theoretical notions of the other institutions the interest group accepts. How might these theoretical notions affect the interest group's calculations? Let us first assume that the bureaucracy is regarded as a fully constrained actor. That is, it simply functions as a transmission belt and implements the policy chosen by Congress. Let us also assume that the courts attempt to implement their most preferred policy. In a situation like this, the interest group will hesitate to place power with the courts and will likely give much leeway to the agency. The logic is that if the group has succeeded in creating a favorable agency, it will feel relatively sure that the agency will implement the policy that Congress (and the group) wants it to implement.

This relative certainty is due to several factors. First, the legislature may have arranged procedures and structures to reflect the preferences of the enacting coalition (McCubbins, Noll, and Weingast 1989). Second, the group may carry strong influence with the current Congress or president and through these other bodies hold a great deal of power over the agency. And finally, the personnel at the agency may be sympathetic to the group's goals.

Combinations and Competition of Approaches

These three approaches obviously are not completely distinct from each other. In some ways they overlap, and in other ways they compete with each other. For example, the legal regime and institutional approaches could compete in the following way. The legal regime might suggest that courts actually have changed their approach from what it was in the previous era (e.g., perhaps they no longer defer so easily to agencies). However, the institutional approach might cause interest groups to believe that this change is superficial; if courts are perceived as dominated by realists

---

25. Legal realism, of course, is much subtler than this. Most important, realism was primarily a reaction to the excessive formalism that preceded it. As a result, the primary argument of realism holds that law is determined in part by exogenous forces.

26. Other theories of court behavior include the argument that courts protect the rights of minorities and the Chicago-school argument that courts choose outcomes that are most economically efficient.

who are interested in trying to implement a specific policy objective, it may be that only the language the courts use to defend their decisions has changed (i.e., as the attitudinal model would suggest, they simply make decisions that are closest to their most-preferred points).

On the other hand, these two approaches also overlap and can reinforce each other. It would be very easy to imagine the legal regime providing a constraint on the institutional model. For example, courts may not be allowed to act in certain ways because of prevailing norms, so the types of decisions, or at least the way they go about reaching decisions (which does, after all, provide constraints), are important for modifying any basic theoretical view of the nature of an institution. Going even further, the legal regime may be used to determine which institutional model is dominant, or appropriate, in any given era.

Similarly, the experiential approach can both compete and overlap with each of the other two approaches. Concrete experience may actually fly in the face of expectations derived from either the norms of the day or general expectations about institutional behavior. On the other hand, the two more abstract approaches may provide information either to those groups that have had experience with courts and agencies but are uncertain about directions these other institutions are likely to take in the future, or to groups that are uncertain whether agencies or courts are friendlier.

Congressional Motivations

Interest groups, of course, are not alone in their attempts to structure judicial review provisions to achieve political advantage. Members of Congress obviously choose from the same set of provisions as do interest groups when considering how to structure judicial review. Provisions like standing, reviewability, burden of proof, and scope of review all affect the probability of certain outcomes obtaining when a case is heard by the courts. And since members of Congress, like interest groups, care about these future outcomes, they pay attention to these procedural details.

The factors that influence interest-group choices also influence the choices made by Congress. Experience, for example, provides a guide to members of Congress in much the same way it informs interest groups. However, the other influences—the interest-group context, the legal regime, and the institutional context—need to be reexamined more closely in light of congressional incentives. In order to understand what Congress does and why, we must understand the motives and incentives of its members, as they may differ from the motives and incentives of interest groups or other political actors.

The Interest-Group Context

First of all, the interest-group context affects the actions and goals of members of Congress. Due to the well-known electoral connection, legislators derive their preferences in part from interest groups. Interest groups provide resources, such as money, staff for campaigns, and the promise of voters, that members can use in their bids for reelection. These resources give interest groups influence over members and make members aware of and finely attuned to the desires of these groups, especially when dealing with arcane procedural details that are not likely to attract the interest of the general public. If they seek reelection, members must heed the demands of these groups. And if interest groups have definite preferences over judicial review, members of Congress need to be aware of these preferences.[27]

While group pressure is undoubtedly a key determinant of congressional behavior, the impact of this pressure should not be overstated.[28] On most issues faced by Congress, there will be interests pushing from different directions, urging the passage of different, and perhaps opposite, types of provisions. This diversity of interests, of course, is not unique to provisions for judicial review but is endemic to the entire legislative process.

Institutions

The second context is institutional. Members of Congress seek power vis-à-vis other political institutions and guard against actions that can erode any sources of power they currently have. In particular, members will try to use judicial review provisions to protect against the loss of power to other institutions, such as opposing political parties, future Congresses, and the Supreme Court.

Party politics may play a role in the determination of which procedures and structures should be established. For example, both party politics and the fear of losing power combined to override the desires of strong

---

27. For a strong view of how members' actions are driven by interest group demands (even on procedural issues), see Moe 1989 and 1990a. Moe takes the position that members of Congress function as little more than conduits for interest-group demands. This position is often associated with early works of pluralism; but much recent work on the interaction between interest groups and Congress disputes the conduit notion and recognizes a more multifaceted relationship (see, e.g., Bauer, Pool, and Dexter 1972; Hayes 1981; Austen-Smith and Wright 1994).

28. For example, Weingast and Marshall (1988) contend that constituents' interests "systematically—though not necessarily completely—affect a congressman's votes" (137, n. 5). Arnold (1990) also argues that members' responsiveness to interest-group demands is less than is commonly believed. See also Maass 1983.

interest groups regarding the Radio Act of 1927. Most radio interests supported placing the regulation of radio in the hands of Herbert Hoover, then the secretary of commerce. However, Democrats in Congress feared that such placement would hurt them in two ways. First, it would aid Hoover, the likely Republican presidential candidate, by giving him control over the valuable new resource of radio. And second, it would extend power to the executive branch at the expense of Congress. Democrats, as a result, were instrumental in placing control of radio in an independent regulatory agency.

In addition, current members of Congress want to constrain future members of Congress (Ferejohn and Weingast 1992). While this notion may seem intuitive, however, a counterargument might run as follows: Members of Congress know that if they choose to run for reelection, they have a high probability of winning. They know that they will be in a position to alter policy in the future. Since they will be pressured by groups at that time, it may seem worthwhile to allow themselves greater input at this future time so they can garner the benefits that would accrue to them from the newly grateful interest groups.

While seemingly logical, this counterargument ignores some important considerations. To begin with, members of Congress often simply seek to avoid controversy (R. Weaver 1986; Moe 1989). While blame shifting may be a transparent strategy (see Horn and Shepsle 1989, 505), there is a difference between shifting blame and avoiding controversy. To the extent that representatives can avoid future controversy by hard-wiring policy during the front end of the process, they will. In addition, even if representatives did not seek to avoid policy controversies in this way, legislation has a higher present value when it assures a longer stream of benefits (Landes and Posner 1975). While groups and members of Congress will discount these future benefits, they remain cognizant that groups will pay a higher price for legislation that yields greater benefits in the current period. Furthermore, if a policy is changed, members cannot be confident that they will be able to move the policy back to its original location (McCubbins, Noll, and Weingast 1989).

Finally, members of Congress are not just competing with future members of Congress. Members are also in competition with the Supreme Court for influence over policy, and throughout the last two centuries there has been a continual ebb and flow of power between these two institutions (Murphy 1962; Lasser 1988). Because of this fluctuation, members must be cognizant of the Supreme Court and its actions.[29]

---

29. Katzmann (1992) argues, however, that members of Congress rarely have enough information about or pay enough attention to the actions of the courts to act in such a foresighted manner.

Congress does have the ability, of course, to influence court decisions. As mentioned in the previous chapter, it might do so through direct or indirect pressure; it might engage in gamesmanship involving the interpretation of statutes (e.g., by inserting statements into the congressional record); or it might, as this study demonstrates, strategically choose the provisions that will guide review. The Supreme Court, however, can independently affect the actions taken by the reviewing courts. And it can do so much more easily than can Congress. The Court simply needs to issue decisions changing the guidelines under which lower courts make decisions. In short, the Court can issue precedents and in doing so directly affect the actions of lower courts.[30]

Congress and the Supreme Court therefore are both participants in a game where, as in all games, the outcome is determined by the actions of both participants. The prize in this game is the lower court decision; while Congress and the Supreme Court both can affect it, both also realize they are involved in an iterative game.

Legal Regime

The legal regime is the final influence on members of Congress as they attempt to design judicial review. Consider, for example, the delegation of responsibility to independent regulatory agencies.[31] In particular, in the period this study focuses on, the legitimacy of independent regulatory agencies was an extraordinarily consequential but largely unsettled question. Members of Congress, the courts, and the executive, as well as the American Bar Association and academics, all questioned the need for and the legitimacy of these agencies.[32]

---

30. On the issue of Supreme Court influence over lower courts, see Cameron, Segal, and Cover 1995; Songer, Segal, and Cameron 1994; and Ulmer 1984.

31. This delegation of responsibility might be seen as part of an institutional struggle, as some members of Congress might be loathe to abdicate responsibility to independent agencies; or it might be seen as an example of how members actually seek good and legitimate policy objectives, rather than simply acting as transmission belts for interest group desires. But as stressed earlier, the three approaches discussed in the text can be thought of as streams of information that might overlap.

32. The *American Bar Association Reports* during the 1920s, for example, routinely criticized the independent-commission format. In 1927, for example, the association's Standing Committee on Air Law wrote in its annual report: "However excellent the work of the present Commission may prove to be, it is the feeling of your committee that the Bar generally should oppose the creation of more federal commissions" (American Bar Association 1927, 233). It was not until the 1930s that opinion on this issue began to shift, as the Bar Association and other observers (e.g., Landis 1938) began issuing a vigorous defense of the independent-commission format.

The views of many members of Congress certainly reflected their awareness of this question and in turn their attitude toward these new creations. Members attacked the general idea of independent commissions and, more specifically, excoriated the Radio Commission.[33] Representative Blanton, for example, issued the following charge: "The great trouble with the hearings of the Federal Radio Commission is that they are before ignorant, inexperienced, incompetent, inefficient examiners" (75 *Congressional Record* 3689 [1932]).

Blanton was not alone in his criticisms. Representative McGugin added the following broadside to the assault on the agency:

> In taking stations off the air they are not taken off in the old-fashioned American way. Under the rules a man who has invested $200,000 in a station has no vested rights. Maybe not. But he does have the right to a fair hearing in the old-fashioned American way, the old-fashioned Anglo-Saxon way, if you please.
>
> He must leave his home State, leave behind the United States district court of his State and come to Washington for his hearing before a commission; and then, after that commission renders its decision his sole right of appeal is to the District of Columbia Court of Appeals. I say that is not American jurisprudence, it is not Anglo-Saxon; it is the same kind of tyranny that was practiced in the thirteen Colonies when our fathers rebelled against being dragged across the sea to London for a hearing. (75 *Congressional Record* 3692 [1932])[34]

Many members who argued that such agencies were in fact not legitimate argued for strong judicial constraints on the actions of such agencies, relying heavily on the arguments that good public policy could not be made by unaccountable agencies.[35] While it would be naive to fail to look beneath the words of such members to see if there were political, as opposed to pol-

---

33. Interest groups added to these criticisms. For example, the president of RCA, General Harbord, issued the following characterization: "[C]ommissions [are] a device for the evasion of responsibility." See testimony of General Harbord in Senate Committee on Interstate Commerce, *Hearings on S. 6,* 71st Cong., 1st sess., 1929, 1328.

34. These and other similarly pointed remarks can be found throughout the pages of the *Congressional Record,* as well as in Cass 1989, 86.

35. In an interesting departure from the Progressive tradition, some scholars even assailed the notion that expertise would enable the agencies to form good policy. E. Pendleton Herring, for example, wrote, "Whatever competence as experts they may possess is of little more than incidental significance in determining policy. *Expertise* can apply only to scientific problems and, while it ensures a grasp of technical limitations and possibilities, it does not contribute to a positive elucidation of the public welfare" (1936, 166).

icy, concerns, the possibility remains that many members were concerned about the ability of regulatory agencies to make good policy.

For all these reasons, members of Congress have cause to be concerned about judicial review of administrative actions. For members of Congress, as for interest groups, the choice of judicial review provisions is determined in part by factors such as interest groups, institutions, experience, and the legal regime. Having established this, we now need to move to a more concrete theoretical understanding of the politics of judicial review.

CHAPTER 3

A Theoretical Look at Judicial Review:
Agencies, Courts, and Uncertainty

Up to now, this analysis has adopted a perspective similar to that of scholars who examined the creation of bureaucratic structures and procedures (e.g., Moe 1989, 1990a, 1990b; McCubbins, Noll, and Weingast 1987, 1989). The central focus has been on the incentives and abilities of political actors to control, or at least constrain, the courts, much as earlier studies focused on the control of agencies. The route has shown that many of the same principles developed in studies of bureaucratic organization can be adapted and applied to the relationship between Congress, interest groups, and the courts.

Because these other models were specifically developed with agencies in mind, care must be taken when using the same concepts in examining other institutions.[1] In other words, these theories cannot be lifted wholesale from the bureaucracy and blindly attached to the courts. Instead, they must reflect the distinctive nature of the court as an institution. Because of the differences between these institutions, members of Congress and interest groups will be guided by different concerns when writing provisions for the courts than when writing such provisions for executive or independent agencies. And in the previous chapter, I suggested that several factors, such as the role of experience, institutional theories, and the legal regime, all affect the choice of judicial review provisions.

An additional perspective can help us structure our thinking about the selection of judicial review provisions. Heretofore, my main focus was on the courts. However, while members of the enacting coalition are concerned with the actions of the courts, their concern is instrumental. What they are ultimately interested in is much more basic—they are interested in obtaining the best possible policy outcome. Whether this outcome results from court action or agency action is irrelevant to them, as long as the final outcome is favorable. In other words, their preferences are not literally over "courts" and "agencies," but rather are over the expected policy out-

---

1. For a debate about the potential problems involved in applying theories developed in one context to other contexts, see Weyland 1995 and Shipan 1995.

comes that will emerge from these institutions. To this end, they do not look simply at controls on courts, or at controls on agencies, but rather at the likely policy outcome. It is the expectations over outcomes that induce preferences over institutions.[2]

Consequently, a related concern has to do with the broader question of the role of agencies and courts in American politics. Instead of just looking at the relationship between interest groups and the courts, or interest groups and the bureaucracy, one needs to focus on preferences over outcomes. In other words, having preferences over judicial review does not indicate preferences over the *location* of decision making alone, but also reflects an *expectation of the outcome* likely to emerge from that location.

Focusing solely on the courts does yield some insights, as did a focus on the bureaucracy in these earlier studies. For example, it shows, as I have mentioned, that judicial review provisions are not simply procedural details. It also draws out the importance of specific factors, such as prior experiences with courts and agencies, that groups and members of Congress will rely on to determine what types of review provisions should be used.

But while this information clearly is important, it begs several important questions. It does not shed much light on *when* political actors will push for certain provisions, and it is not specific enough in explaining *why* they push for certain provisions. More generally, what are the conditions under which members of Congress will prefer broad judicial review to review conceived more narrowly? While it is necessary to realize that review provisions are important, in order to truly understand them we must be able to address these questions, as it is not clear that political actors always will be in a position to choose such provisions strategically. By focusing on both the courts and agencies, I hope to gain some purchase on these questions.

How might such questions be addressed? One method would be purely inductive. For instance, one could choose to focus on a certain policy area, study all the laws that have been passed in this area, look at the differences over time in the specification of judicial review provisions, and attempt to draw some conclusions from the cases. One might also compare the types of provisions enacted in different eras. Another comparative tactic would be to focus on a specific era and compare provisions across policy areas, perhaps finding that something specific to each type of policy has an effect on the choice of provisions.

---

2. And, as I will stress later, members of the enacting coalition need to look at these two institutions in conjunction, rather than in isolation, when trying to ascertain where to vest final policy-making authority.

While such an approach has limitations, and care must be taken to ensure that cases are chosen well and that the generalizations drawn from each set of case studies are not exaggerated, it certainly can be a productive and worthwhile way of studying issues such as this (e.g., A. George 1979; G. King, Keohane, and Verba 1994). Clearly, however, an inductive approach is not the only feasible method. In the following sections, I will utilize a more deductive approach in addressing these questions.

Two variables will be of central importance. The first is the outcome each of these institutions can be expected to produce. Political actors will use whatever information they possess to form expectations about future outcomes. I have suggested that they will rely on some combination of experience, legal regime, and institutional theories, along with an awareness of the goals of opposing interests. All are sources of information about what outcome to expect.

In the front end of the policy process, therefore, the members of the enacting coalition will form expectations about the likely outcome of vesting final review in the courts and will compare those predictions to the expectation derived from vesting final review in the agency. And the coalition will, for obvious reasons, prefer having an outcome closer to its ideal point.

However, a second variable that also comes into play here is *uncertainty*. While interest groups and legislators may be able to form expectations about outcomes, their expectations also are surrounded by an immense amount of uncertainty. The amount of uncertainty will have an effect on the calculation of members.[3] Thus, not only the expected outcome from each institution, but also the uncertainty surrounding each institution, will enter into the calculations of political actors.

Previous Studies

In studying the relationship among the different branches of government, several approaches have been used. Some studies, for example, focus on *why* Congress has chosen to delegate decision-making authority to agencies. For the purposes of this analysis, however, more important are the studies that focus on *how* such decision making, once delegated, can be controlled by other political actors.

While analyses of this latter sort have grown in number and in detail, they have rarely included a detailed analysis of the role played by the courts. McCubbins, Noll, and Weingast (1989) discuss the repercussions

---

3. Uncertainty about outcomes can be thought of as the variance surrounding the expected value. The shape of the probability distribution is also likely to be important (Fiorina 1986).

of a court-induced shift from the status quo; Moe (1989) argues that both powerful and weak interest groups will have an incentive to open agency decision making up to scrutiny by the courts; and Mashaw (1985) argues that the presence of the courts may cause delegation of policy-making authority to be more optimal. But while these and other studies do acknowledge the presence of the judiciary, discussions of the courts tend to be somewhat peripheral to their main concerns.[4]

One analyst to focus specifically on the role of the courts is Fiorina, who has written a trio of articles dealing with this subject (1982, 1985, 1986). In these articles, Fiorina addresses several questions concerning the nature of congressional delegation of regulatory authority. A predominant question in these papers is whether members of Congress will prefer to delegate responsibility to an agency or will instead prefer to have the courts review whether the behavior of regulated firms is in accordance with laws passed by Congress. As he later characterizes his argument, the choice between regulation-by-administration and court-enforced regulation can be viewed as choosing between relatively less certain and more certain alternatives. In his models, which rely on a combination of historical, political, and economic analyses, he explores the conditions under which either one or the other type of regulation is chosen.

In examining this choice, Fiorina acknowledges and emphasizes the relevance and importance of what he terms "historical awareness." He writes:

> If we believe, as I do, that institutions matter, the changing character of our national legislature suggests that our theorizing about its choice of policy instruments should proceed against a backdrop of historical awareness. (1982, 35)[5]

---

4. Noll and Shimada explicitly include the courts: "Another aspect of bureaucratic structure that influences performance is the extent to which agency decisions can be reviewed by courts. The use of judicial review is far more common in the United States than in other countries. Judicial interpretations of the constitutional principles of due process, equal protection, and separation of power cause few decisions to be beyond the reach of judicial review. Nevertheless, agencies differ substantially in the intensity, frequency, and substance of judicial review that their authorizing legislation requires" (1991, 224). Also see McCubbins, Noll, and Weingast 1992; Ferejohn and Weingast 1992; Spiller 1992b; Spiller and Tiller 1996; and the discussion of Macey 1992a in chapter 7.

5. Fiorina carefully includes the following caveat: "Admittedly, there is a danger here. While a model which ignores the detail of the legislative process may be inherently incapable of enlightening us about legislative outcomes, a model which incorporates too much detail may provide a good accounting of the Occupational Safety and Health Act of 1970 (OSHA) but not of the Federal Communications Act of 1934 (FCC), or the Interstate Commerce Act of 1887 (ICC)" (1982, 35).

He goes on to add that

> There is yet another reason to bear in mind the history of regulatory politics in the United States. Though social scientists hesitate to admit historical experience as an explanatory fact in their models, *the regulatory debate at any particular time clearly reflects historical experience.* We can translate the relevant considerations into more congenial terms—the use of historical experience to reduce uncertainty, for example—but current calculations incorporate historical experience just the same. (1982, 35; emphasis added)

Fiorina is absolutely correct in his insistence on using historical evidence to understand regulation, which can most profitably be understood as a product of broader political and social currents (Rabin 1986). More generally, historical evidence can shed much light on a variety of political phenomena. And as emphasized in chapter 2, our understanding of judicial review also can benefit from taking into account historical factors, such as experience and the legal regime.

However, while Fiorina's articles, with their use of historical, economic, and institutional analyses, have yielded several important insights, they also present an incomplete picture of the process. Members of Congress certainly do try to decide which forum is likely to be "better" for them, which forum is likely to yield greater political benefits. But the question runs deeper than he allows and is not simply a question of agencies versus courts. The key point is this: Courts are involved in *both* of these scenarios. That is, even if Congress (or another political actor) prefers to vest policy-making authority in agencies, it also must realize that the courts still can have some influence on the eventual policy outcome.

Fiorina does not neglect this point, but, drawing on his historical analysis, he does question its relevance and argues that it reflects a limited perspective on the role of courts and agencies. After contending that the split between courts and agencies is not a false dichotomy, he goes on to address these two types of delegation as conceptually distinct—Congress either delegates policy-making authority to an agency or determines that courts should be the enforcers of regulatory statutes.

Fiorina's main point is well taken—there unquestionably are some important conceptual differences between these two types of policy-making. His argument on this point is worth quoting at length:

> This dichotomization of the administrative and legal systems is an admitted oversimplification. In contemporary America the enforcement of few laws is left entirely to the initiative of the individual liti-

gant; administrative involvement is the rule. Conversely, even where the administrative system has primary responsibility for the enforcement of a statute, the courts loom in the background. Some would contend that this reality vitiates the usefulness of the distinction I have drawn.

I am sensitive to such arguments but would offer two comments in reply. First, the arguments reflect a contemporary, if not an ahistorical perspective. At one time the dichotomy was clearly perceived and was the basis for major political conflict. . . . If, as the years went by, delegation of legislative power to administrators became easier (i.e., less controversial), and seemingly more natural, the historical question remains: what factors led to increased reliance on the administrative process? Second, even if historical evidence of a political choice between administrative and legal forms of regulation were not in evidence, the logical question would remain: why not attempt to regulate without reliance on bureaucratic entities? (1982, 36, n. 5)

I will not directly engage in this debate here. Instead, I will take as given that Congress has already decided to delegate responsibility to an agency. However, it is essential to remember that once this decision has been made, courts *still* can play a role. In other words, once the agency makes a decision, often this decision can be appealed to the courts. The question, then, is whether the enacting coalition wants the agency to have free run of the policy area, or whether it wants to add another procedural layer—the courts—on top of the agency. It is to this question I will turn shortly.[6]

Before doing so, however, I should point out another important approach that can be used as a building block, an approach found in the work of McCubbins (1985) and McCubbins and Page (1987). There are two reasons for turning to these studies. First, while many analyses of regulation—including Fiorina's—focus on the question of whether to delegate, McCubbins and Page instead take off from the point at which the decision to delegate already has been made. Second, in seeking to explain the nature of delegation, they rely heavily on the role played by uncertainty.

McCubbins and Page note that when Congress delegates to an agency, a conflict may exist between the goals and aspirations of Congress and those of the agency. In such a situation, Congress cannot simply

---

6. Again, Fiorina is addressing the question of how members of Congress decide between delegating to an agency or relying on the courts, whereas I am asking a slightly different question, which is: Once Congress has decided to delegate to an agency, to what extent does it also allow the courts into the picture?

impose its will on the agency—the instruments of control are imperfect, as is congressional information about agency actions.[7] Because of these limitations, one of the fundamental problems Congress faces in delegating responsibility is the amount of uncertainty.[8]

Legislators are uncertain about the details of the policy area, the potential costs of controlling the activity to be regulated, their ability to control the implementation of their chosen policy, and the true preferences and powers of interest groups. Based on these factors, these authors examine how changes in uncertainty will affect the regulatory scope, procedures, or substantive discretion delegated to an agency. For the purposes of this study, what is important is the emphasis placed on the variable nature of delegation (once the decision to delegate has been made) and the emphasis on uncertainty about outcomes and institutions.[9]

Courts, Agencies, and Judicial Review

Each of these studies takes us part of the way to answering questions about when, why, and under what conditions Congress and interest groups will make use of judicial review provisions. What we need now is to combine the approaches of each—drawing on Fiorina's example in paying attention to a mixture of historical, political, and economic approaches, and for his recognition that different outcomes are likely to emerge from courts and agencies; and drawing on McCubbins and Page for the centrality of uncertainty and the variable nature of delegation.

Following are several propositions about the specification of judicial review provisions, propositions that reflect a combination of economic, institutional, and historical approaches. All of the following proceed from the central assumption of this chapter—that political actors have preferences over policy outcomes. They also have preferences over which institutions will be involved in creating policy, but these institutional preferences are induced by the preferences over outcomes. Political actors, therefore, will view institutions as means by which preferred policy outcomes may be achieved. The theoretical propositions are as follows:

---

7. The authors vividly compare the problem of controlling an agency to "walking a dog with a rubber leash on a dark night" (1987, 410). Since the leash is not rigid, control is weak to begin with and is made even more difficult by not being able to see well in the dark (i.e., congressional controls over agencies, weak to begin with, are weakened still further by the paucity of information about what the agency is doing).

8. The second fundamental problem is conflict, which arises because legislators represent different districts with different interests.

9. For a similar combination of delegation and uncertainty, albeit in a different context, see Bawn 1995. See also Epstein and O'Halloran 1994.

PROPOSITION 1. *With perfect and complete information about the preferences of courts and agencies, political actors will favor vesting final authority in the institution that is likely to produce the best outcome. In addition, Congress may allow review along some dimensions but not along other dimensions.*

PROPOSITION 2. *Information about the preferences of courts and agencies is not likely to be perfect or complete, and political actors therefore will be faced with uncertainty about the outputs of these other institutions. This uncertainty can affect the assignment of final authority.*

PROPOSITION 3. *The amount of uncertainty over the actions of the courts and the bureaucracy is not necessarily equal.*

PROPOSITION 4. *When the amount of uncertainty over the actions of the courts and the bureaucracy is* not *equal, actors' preferences will depend on the nature and the shape of the distribution.*

Now that I have listed each of the theoretical propositions, in the following sections I will consider each of them in detail.

PROPOSITION 1. *With perfect and complete information about the preferences of courts and agencies, political actors will favor vesting final authority in the institution that is likely to produce the best outcome. In addition, Congress may allow review along some dimensions but not along other dimensions.*

Let us begin with a world of perfect information and a single policy dimension on which the agency, the judiciary, and Congress each have some preferred point, denoted by A, J, and C, respectively.[10] In the game played by these three actors, the judiciary has the last move.[11] Thus, Congress delegates decision-making authority to the agency and chooses whether to allow judicial review of agency decisions; the agency picks a policy; and the judiciary, if permitted, reviews the agency's choice.

One can conceive of judicial review of agency actions in two distinct ways.[12] First, the judiciary may be able to specify a new policy. In this sce-

10. While I refer to *Congress* in this discussion, one can also think of Congress as representing the preferences of the enacting coalition, including the interested groups. To simplify matters, I ignore the internal institutions of Congress, such as the committee system.

11. I recognize that this assumption differs from that made in most other separation-of-powers games and briefly discuss it at the end of this section.

12. For similar discussions, see Spiller 1992a, Shipan 1993, and Cameron 1993.

nario, the court, acting as a *policy selector,* may choose to overrule the agency and implement *J,* its most preferred policy. Second, the judiciary may not be able to implement *J,* but instead may determine only whether the agency's policy should stand. In other words, the court acts as a *policy gatekeeper,* and if it chooses to overrule the policy, the policy outcome will revert back to the status quo, which I will call *q.*

Different policy outcomes will result under these two scenarios. In figure 3.1a, for example, Congress will prefer to allow judicial review. Prohibition of judicial review would yield a policy at *A;* allowing for review yields a policy of *J,* which Congress prefers.[13]

Outcomes are not limited to *J* and *A* when the judiciary acts as a policy gatekeeper. If the judiciary allows the agency's policy choice to stand, the outcome will be *A;* but if it overrules the agency, policy will revert to the status quo. Furthermore, if the agency acts strategically, it will take into account the judiciary's preferences and, if possible, will try to avoid being overturned on review by choosing some point *z* such that $|z - J| < |q - J|$ and also such that $|z - A| < |q - A|$ (see fig. 3.1b). In other words, the agency will choose some point that both it and the judiciary prefer to the status quo.

The two scenarios thus lead to different outcomes. In the first scenario, the outcome can be either *A* or *J,* whereas a wide range of outcomes

(a)

(b)

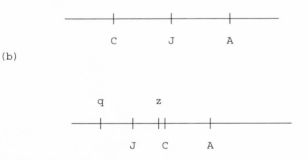

Fig. 3.1.   Alternative judicial roles; (a) policy selector; (b) policy gatekeeper

13. Even when preferences are arrayed such that $J < C < A$, Congress will vest final authority with the institution closest to its own preferences. It may seem that the agency could offer to choose some policy that Congress, as well as the agency, prefers to *J.* The important point to recognize is that it is only the existence of judicial review that would force it to do so. Note, however, that I am not allowing for the possibility of a congressional response.

can occur in the second scenario. But while the set of potential outcomes may be different, the behavior of Congress is the same—it will seek to vest final authority such that the policy outcome is closest to its most-preferred point.[14] In either case, however, if the judiciary is closer to Congress than is the agency, Congress will prefer to bequeath broad powers of review to the judiciary.[15] The essential point is that Congress can assign judicial review strategically in order to obtain the most favorable outcome possible.

A Policy Selector in Two Dimensions

While this simple model provides a useful start, most agencies do not operate in a one-dimensional world. Not surprisingly, when we do introduce a second dimension, along with such standard assumptions as Euclidean preferences, similar results obtain. Under conditions of perfect and complete information, members of Congress can use judicial review to achieve more preferable outcomes. They generally will choose to vest final policy-making authority in the hands of the institution that has preferences closest to those of Congress along each dimension.

Take, for example, the first scenario, wherein the judiciary functions as a policy selector. When more than one dimension is considered, the key point to remember is that judicial review is not an all-or-nothing affair. That is, Congress does not have to choose between prohibiting review and allowing full review, but instead can—and does—choose *intermediate levels* of review.

Figure 3.2 demonstrates this point. C, J, and A once again represent the ideal points of Congress, the judiciary, and the agency, respectively. In addition, preferences are configured so that the vertical distance between C and J is less than that between C and A, but the horizontal difference is greater. That is, $|C_y - J_y| < |C_y - A_y|$, but $|C_x - J_x| > |C_x - A_x|$. In this situa-

---

14. Faced with a policy selector court, Congress will always vest final authority with the institution closest to its own preferences; faced with a policy gatekeeper, it will generally (but not always) do the same. The major exception to this situation is when $A - C < J - C$, $A < C < J$, and q takes on extreme values or falls in the interval $(A, C(A))$, where $C(A) = 2C - A$. Judicial review in this case brings policy closer to C. Thus, judicial review is likely to be more prevalent when the judiciary is a policy gatekeeper. Interestingly, since a policy gatekeeper has more limited power than a policy selector, this finding implies that a court that acts in a more limited fashion is more likely to receive the power to review.

15. That is true even in figure 3.1b, where z, the point strategically chosen by the agency, is closer to C than is J. Again, the agency would choose z only because of the existence of judicial review.

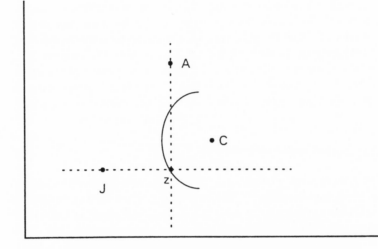

Fig. 3.2.   Judiciary as a policy selector in two dimensions

tion, Congress will allow vertical review (i.e., it will permit the courts to review the agency's actions regarding the vertical policy dimension). At the same time, however, Congress will want to *prohibit* horizontal review. Given a distribution of preferences such as those in figure 3.2, the outcome will be z (the intersection of lines that pass through A and J and are parallel to the axes).[16] Congress prefers z to A, which results from no review, and to J, which results from full review. Thus, Congress may want the courts to review along some dimensions but not others.[17]

As an example, consider an agency that performs two functions—setting technology standards and setting performance standards. Congress may have confidence that the agency will require industry to reach performance standards that Congress itself agrees with, but at the same time, it may not trust the agency to set standards for the adoption of new technologies. On the other hand, Congress may trust the courts to set technology standards but not performance standards. In such a case, Congress

---

16. With intermediary levels of review—vertical or horizontal review—and a two-dimensional model, the outcome will always be along either a vertical or a horizontal line drawn through A.

17. Separability by dimension demonstrates the key point that groups do not view judicial review as a no-lose option, where review always is seen as a second chance to obtain a more favorable outcome at little risk. Here, Congress and the groups it favors are unquestionably made better off by limiting some types of judicial review and allowing others.

could allow judicial review of only the agency's technology standards. In other words, Congress will prefer to allow review over the dimension along which it is closest to the judiciary and to limit review along the other dimension.

A Policy Gatekeeper in Two Dimensions

As we saw earlier, however, the scenario wherein the judiciary may only return policy to the status quo (rather than implementing a new point of its choosing) can result in different outcomes. We now need to examine this situation to determine whether similar outcomes obtain even if we adopt the (arguably more realistic) assumption that courts function as policy gatekeepers—that is, when courts overrule an agency, the policy reverts back to q, the status quo.[18]

The details of this model are presented in appendix A, where the interested reader may consult them. The results of the model, however, can be summarized easily. In figure 3.3, two perpendicular dotted lines bisect the region between the ideal points of the judiciary and the agency.[19] What is most important is which of the quadrants Congress is located in. If Congress is closer to J along both dimensions, it prefers full review; if it is closer to A along both dimensions, it generally prefers no review; and if it is closer to J along only one dimension, it generally prefers to allow review along that dimension only. The results mirror those found in one dimension: by strategically assigning judicial review, Congress can obtain more favorable outcomes.

Advancing the Model

What would happen if other details were included in this two-dimensional model? For example, what would happen if some institutional characteristics, such as the committee system in Congress and the ability of Congress to override court or agency actions, were included? Would logic still reveal that Congress generally prefers to vest authority in the institution with preferences closest to its own?

These are difficult questions, and while I will not tackle them in this study, this model shows the direction in which future work should move. More specifically, outcomes with and without court review should be compared within a more detailed and realistic institutional setting. Intuition indicates, however, that no matter how much detail or "realism" is intro-

---

18. This examination extends into two dimensions some of the ideas found in Gely and Spiller 1990; Ferejohn and Shipan 1990; and Spiller and Gely 1992.

19. The other lines are discussed in appendix A.

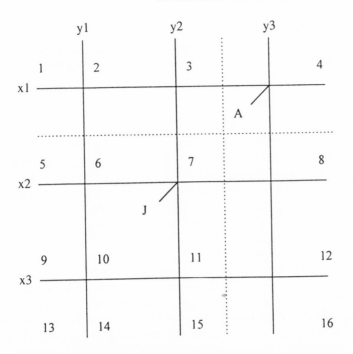

Fig. 3.3. Judiciary as a policy gatekeeper in two dimensions. *A* is located at *x1* ∩ *y3*; *J* is located at *x2* ∩ *y2*.

duced into the model, Congress still will be able to use judicial review to affect policy outcomes. Some supporting evidence for this notion can be found in Ferejohn and Shipan 1990, which demonstrates that judicial review has the effect of increasing the responsiveness of policy outcomes to the current Congress. Alternatively, Ferejohn and Weingast (1992) show that under certain conditions, judicial review also can increase the responsiveness of policy outcomes to the desires of the Congress that originally created the policy. And finally, Landes and Posner (1975) have argued that one result of having an independent judiciary is that such a system increases the benefits of legislation to interest groups by enforcing the statutory bargain. This also benefits current members of Congress, as the increased value of the legislation implies that they are able to extract a higher price from the groups.

Finally, a more realistic model might allow Congress to overturn the court's decision. Thus, the agency and the court also would have to take into account congressional preferences when choosing a policy. However, given that legislation is not costless and knowledge of other actors' preferences is not perfect, even if Congress has the power to overturn bureaucratic decisions and judicial rulings, it still prefers to structure procedures in such a manner that the policy is as close as possible to its ideal point, thereby reducing costs of legislating. Once again, we would expect to find that members of the enacting coalition would want to vest final authority in the institution that is likely to produce the most-preferred outcome.

PROPOSITION 2. *Information about the preferences of courts and agencies is not likely to be perfect or complete, and political actors therefore will be faced with uncertainty about the outputs of these other institutions. This uncertainty can affect the assignment of final authority.*

All students of politics—even those who employ models of perfect information—acknowledge that in the real world there is a great deal of uncertainty about political outcomes and actions. Indeed, the concept of uncertainty is central to many recent models of politics. Yet while commonly used in explanations of politics, uncertainty can mean different things to different people. For the argument I am making, let me start with the obvious observation that members of interest groups or Congress cannot know with certainty what outcomes will result from agencies or courts. That is, once decision-making authority is delegated to these other institutions, the expected outcome is uncertain.[20]

That uncertainty surrounds bureaucratic outcomes should not come as a surprise to anyone. In the terms of the principal-agent literature, for example, it is acknowledged that bureaucracies do not act as perfect agents. Both slippage and shirking can lead to outcomes that Congress opposes.[21] In terms of the more sociologically oriented literature on organizations, it is clear that factors such as goal displacement can lead agencies to produce outcomes that Congress did not plan on. Wilson (1980, 1990) and many of his students (e.g., S. Weaver 1980; Katzmann 1980) also have ably pointed out that many factors internal to agencies—most notably, the types of people populating the agency—will have a large impact on the outcome. All of these and other factors reinforce the notion that agency actions will be impossible to predict with certainty.

Court actions may be even more difficult to predict than are the actions of agencies. To begin with, unlike many agencies, courts are not set up to be agents of the legislature, so there is much less reason to suspect that these courts are going to act in accordance with what legislators want.[22] But

---

20. This observation parallels Gilligan and Krehbiel's (1989, 1990) and Krehbiel's (1991) argument that outcomes are a function of policy choices plus a stochastic term.

21. *Slippage* denotes an unintentional deviation, whereas *shirking* is an intentional deviation.

22. On this point, see the discussion in chapters 1 and 2 on the limits of controls over courts.

beyond that, there are often great disparities between courts at *different* levels (e.g., state versus federal courts), *within* levels (e.g., the different appeals courts usually are dissimilar), and finally, across time (e.g., the Supreme Court in 1980 was very different from the Supreme Court in 1960). All these differences make it difficult to talk about "the judiciary," without even getting into the problems of trying to predict what it will do.[23]

While the foregoing discussion is necessarily brief, the essential point is easily made. Both agencies and courts are complex organizations, and it is impossible to know with certainty what actions they will take. That, again, is the central idea behind much of the literature on agencies. If outcomes were predictable, then the impact of asymmetric information, for example, would be less severe for the principal.

Members of Congress simply cannot foresee what other policy questions will arise in the future. If they could, the problems of agency would disappear, and members would write into law the ways in which the agency should deal with all future contingencies. However, since that is not possible, members of Congress need to write into law the structures and procedures that will guide agencies and courts to the decisions the enacting coalition would prefer.

Finally, it is important to realize that uncertainty about future outcomes can derive from two sources. First, as has been emphasized here, members of the enacting coalition will seek to mitigate problems of bureaucratic drift. That is, they will use structures and procedures to attempt to reduce the amount of slippage and shirking by the bureaucracy.

However, this uncertainty is only one problem that the enacting coalition must worry about. Another equally important problem is what Shepsle (1992) refers to as "coalitional drift" and Moe (1989) labels "political uncertainty." Members of the enacting coalition not only must worry about the potential problems of delegating responsibility to an agency; they also must realize that future members of Congress may have preferences that differ from the preferences of the enacting coalition.

Thus, the notion of uncertainty over outcomes is clear. In the case of an agency, even though Congress has delegated responsibility, it cannot completely control the agency. And, as discussed in other chapters, in the case of the courts, there is even less control. While in both cases members of Congress and interest groups might be able to make good guesses about what these other institutions will do, some uncertainty is unavoidable.[24]

---

23. Shepsle's 1990 dictum that Congress is a "they," not an "it," could apply to the judiciary as well as to Congress.

24. Again, as discussed in the previous chapter, groups and members of Congress think about the expected utility of each provision, where expected utility is calculated as follows: $EU(j_i) = p(j_i)v_j(j_i) + (1 - p(j_i))v_a$. Uncertainty enters here about the values of both judicial and bureaucratic actions (v_j and v_a, respectively).

The Effect of Uncertainty

Figures 3.4a and 3.4b show simple single-dimensional models that present examples of how uncertainty can cause Congress to make choices that differ from what it would do under conditions of perfect information.[25] First, reviewing the case of perfect information, we see in figure 3.4a that if the courts are allowed to review the agency's decision, the agency will choose z. Since Congress prefers A (the point that will result if review is not allowed for) to z, it will not allow the judiciary to review the agency's decision.

The next figure, however, shows that uncertainty about the preferences of these other institutions can affect the choice made by Congress. In figure 3.4b, Congress knows only that the court is located somewhere between J_1 and J_2.[26] Congress also knows that if the court is located at J_1, judicial review would cause the agency to choose z_1, whereas if it were located at J_2, the agency would choose z_2.[27] Since Congress clearly prefers z_1 to A, but also clearly prefers A to z_2, its decision will be determined by its expectation of J's true location. If it believes (or is convinced) that the judiciary is located at J_1, then it would, in contrast to the complete information model, want the court to review the agency's policy decisions.[28] Thus, uncertainty over the actions of the judiciary potentially could change the assignment of authority.[29]

PROPOSITION 3. *The amount of uncertainty over the actions of the courts and the bureaucracy is not necessarily equal.*

This proposition is probably the central insight gained from a historical perspective on the role of the courts in the regulatory system. And it

25. Note that these figures deal only with cases in which Congress is located in the area between the two institutions. Except in cases of extreme uncertainty, if Congress were located to the right of J, it would prefer to allow judicial review, and if it were located to the left of A, it would prefer to limit review. Note also that in this section I assume the judiciary is a policy gatekeeper.

26. Only the court knows its true location.

27. $C(A)$ and A are equidistant from C; z_1 and q are equidistant from J_1; and z_2 and q are equidistant from J_2.

28. More generally, Congress prefers to allow judicial review if $z < C(A)$.

29. It should be noted that doing so would give the court the incentive to convince Congress that its location is J_1. Similarly, the agency would have an incentive to convince Congress that it was of a certain "type." See Ferejohn and Shipan 1989 for a relevant discussion of "nice" and "tough" committees.

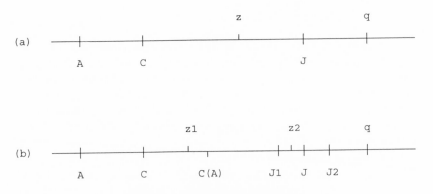

Fig. 3.4. The effects of uncertainty

is not something that is accounted for in existing models of regulation or politics in general.[30] Rather, an appreciation of this inequality can be gained only through looking at historical, anecdotal, and empirical evidence. In particular, the legal regime, as discussed in the previous chapter, will shed light on the amount on uncertainty regarding the actions of each institution.

In general, as intimated in the previous proposition, uncertainty about court actions will be greater than uncertainty about agency actions. There are several reasons for this disparity, many of which have been discussed already. In general, courts are harder to predict because of a lack of political influence over their actions, because it is often not known which courts—or even which judges—will hear appeals, and because of uncertainty about a court's biases.[31]

This generalization, however, is not always true. In the case of broadcasting, for example, it is evident that in 1927 commercial broadcasters had far more confidence in the courts than in the soon-to-be-created agency. As Le Duc and McCain (1970) have noted,

---

30. As indicated earlier in this chapter, one notable exception is Fiorina 1986. In this article, Fiorina shows how differently shaped distributions can affect Congress's choice between a court and an agency as the arbiter of regulation.

31. The tendency of different courts to have different biases is well known. See, for example, Melnick's 1983 account of how interest groups learn which courts are likely to be favorable and which ones they should avoid. Temin (1987, 265) similarly refers to the "careful legal dancing" by parties that were trying to modify the 1956 Consent Decree governing AT&T's actions. Although these parties ultimately failed in this goal, it was not for lack of trying to choose the most favorable forum.

The Radio Act of 1927, which created the Federal Radio Commission (FRC) as an independent regulatory agency, was a far more daring legal experiment than generally has been recognized. . . . *This was an era when most legal scholars still viewed administrative regulation as an evil growth upon the body politic,* threatening common law justice with its alien blend of legislative and judicial power. (393, emphasis added)

Agencies in general were an unknown quantity, and the FRC was no exception.

At the same time, the judiciary was still fully clothed in its role as the protector of property rights.[32] For the most part, this role was still considered part of the Lochner era of the Supreme Court's attitude toward regulation.[33] And as we will see, radio station owners felt a strong need for some form of government regulation. But they also were extremely apprehensive about the potential downside of an independent regulatory commission.

Owners of stations therefore had two options with respect to the agency. First, they could have tried to dictate the exact terms of regulation by writing a very specific and detailed act.[34] Alternately, they could have allowed the commission wide latitude and then followed up with detailed provisions for review. As we will see, the latter course was followed.

PROPOSITION 4. *When the amount of uncertainty over the actions of the courts and the bureaucracy is* not *equal, actors' preferences will depend on the nature and the shape of the distribution.*

---

32. Rabin (1986, 1193) writes: "More clearly than the political branches, the courts assumed the mantle of guardian of market authority until midway through the New Deal. In concrete terms, this meant that the Supreme Court consistently questioned the legitimacy of newly established regulatory programs. But its resistance to change was guarded: Rather than striking down Populist and Progressive era federal regulatory schemes, the Court was inclined to construe agency powers as narrowly as considerations of its own continuing credibility seemed to permit." He goes on to note that while the Court remained committed to private property rights, it was mostly concerned with the legitimacy of regulation and later with controlling administrative discretion.

33. *Lochner v. New York,* 198 U.S. 45 (1905). A more detailed discussion of the importance of this case and the role of property rights can be found in chapter 2.

34. The agency's mandate was especially broad due to information constraints. Because of the extremely fast-changing nature of the technology, groups and members of Congress did not want to lock the commission into positions that would soon become outmoded. Therefore, the agency was given extremely wide latitude, wide enough that an act originally written to cover the allocation of the radio spectrum proved resilient and adaptable enough to cover television, satellites, cable television, and other new developments.

The distribution of outcomes from courts and agencies is not always equal; there can be a great deal of difference in the amount of uncertainty surrounding each institution. If the difference is great enough, it can cause the enacting coalition to depart from the choices it would make under conditions of perfect and complete information.

The impact of different distributions is perhaps easiest to conceive of when $J = A$. If that is the case and there is no variance surrounding these preferences, Congress clearly will be indifferent between the two institutions. However, if there is variance surrounding the one institution but not the other, Congress, being risk-averse, will prefer to cast its lot with the institution whose outcome is surrounded by less variance.[35] It will prefer the outcome around which there is less uncertainty.

The nature of the variance remains important even in situations where there is uncertainty surrounding the choices of *both* the courts and the agency. Again, the easiest case to discuss is the aforementioned one where $A = J$. If $\mathrm{var}(A) > \mathrm{var}(J)$, then Congress would prefer to allow the courts to review the actions of the agency. More interestingly, even when $|C - A| < |C - J|$, if $\mathrm{var}(A) > \mathrm{var}(J)$, then Congress may still prefer to set up provisions that allow the courts to review the agency's actions.

Conceptually, the logic here is equivalent to the use in statistical estimations of the mean squared error (MSE). In choosing estimators, it is not always appropriate to choose the estimator with the least bias; nor is it always appropriate to choose the estimator with the least variance. Instead, one must take into account which estimator has the best combination of small bias and small variance. In other words, one chooses the estimator that minimizes the MSE, where MSE = (variance of the estimator) + (bias of the estimator)^2, or, more technically,

$$\mathrm{MSE}(Y) = E[(Y - Q)^2] = \mathrm{var}(Y) + [b_Y(Q)]^2$$

where $b_Y(Q) = E(Y) - Q$ is the bias (D. Berry and Lindgren 1990, 414; Wonnacutt and Wonnacutt 1984, 197).

The similarity is clear—one can think of Congress as being the "true value" and the preferences of the other institutions as being the estimators. Congress, in deciding between the two institutions, needs to look at both the variance surrounding each institution and that institution's "bias." Since both terms come into play, two results become clear. First, if the "bias" of both institutions is the same, then Congress will seek to place

---

35. The logic is the same as that of a risk-averse actor who prefers some outcome x to a lottery that, on average, yields x.

authority with the institution with the smaller variance. Second, even if one institution yields a less biased estimate (i.e., a more favorable outcome), that institution may have a variance that is sufficiently larger than the other institution's variance that this larger variance outweighs the benefits of the less biased estimate, thereby compelling Congress to place final authority with the other institution.

Conclusion

Through this series of propositions, we have explored the conditions under which Congress and interest groups will seek to allow or prevent judicial review. I have gone beyond the theoretical discussion in the previous chapter and have provided a logic that details the circumstances under which political actors will seek to provide for varying amounts of judicial review. Playing a primary role here is the notion of uncertainty—uncertainty about the average policy preferences of the other institutions and uncertainty about the distributions of these preferences. All else equal, a reduction in the amount of uncertainty surrounding the location of an institution increases the probability that Congress will vest final authority with that institution.

The discussion in this chapter also relates to the examination of review provisions in chapter 2. In that chapter, I argued that the groups and members of Congress would select provisions j_1 rather than j_2 if $EU(j_1) > EU(j_2)$, where $EU(j_i) = p(j_i)v_j(j_i) + (1 - p(j_i))v_a$. Furthermore, I argued that groups and members of Congress make use of several sources of information in trying to determine which provisions to use.

In light of that discussion and the discussion of the propositions in this chapter, three additional points need to be made. First and foremost, members of Congress can use the types of provisions discussed in chapter 2 to reduce uncertainty about judicial outcomes. One way they can do so is by specifying the court (or courts) of review to reduce the amount of uncertainty about a decision. For example, if a group has had favorable substantive experience with a particular court, or if members of Congress know that a specific court has certain leanings, this knowledge can be put to use in reducing the amount of uncertainty surrounding the actions of the judiciary. Thus, by choosing a specific court, Congress can influence the value of v_j, the value of the expected court decision.

Second, giving standing to a group—or denying it to the group's opponents—increases the value of the review provisions to that group. The value specified in the foregoing equation is heavily contingent on whether the group has standing. Standing also has the effect of increasing the likelihood that the courts will choose a favorable outcome because, as discussed in chapter 2, such a provision controls the sources and type of information available to the courts.

Third, increasing the scope of review or the amount of reviewability increases the probability of review, as expressed by $p(j_i)$. Groups and members of Congress can affect the value of a set of provisions by influencing the likelihood of court involvement. And they also can write provisions that determine the extent to which an agency's decision is "open" to judicial review.

CHAPTER 4

Interest Groups and the Origins of Broadcast Regulation

In previous chapters I have explored the reasons why groups and members of Congress will be likely to pay careful attention to legislative details that specify the nature and amount of judicial review. The approach has been primarily theoretical. In the next three chapters I take a different approach. In these substantive chapters I look at the politics of communications policy in the 1920s and 1930s, culminating in an examination of the review provisions discussed in the Communications Act of 1934, in order to test the theoretical argument presented in the preceding chapters.

Before delving into an examination of the review provisions, in the first of the substantive chapters I provide a look at the history of broadcast regulation, focusing on the role of interest groups in general and the National Association of Broadcasters (NAB) in particular. The primary purpose of this discussion is to provide the background for using the case to illustrate the importance of judicial review provisions to interest groups. But there is also a secondary purpose, one that is important for my argument but may be of more interest to scholars with a specific interest in the development of the communications industry. In tracing through these early developments, I hope to establish that while many studies of the early history of broadcasting focus heavily on the tensions between commercial and noncommercial stations, also important was the division between existing and potential stations. An awareness and understanding of this division is essential to understanding the preferences of these groups.[1]

General Background of Radio Regulation

When federal regulation of radio comes into the news these days, it is frequently for the wrong reasons. AM radio, which for decades dominated

---

1. I do not mean to imply that existing stations regularly presented a unified front. Any reading of the battles over patent pooling, antitrust, or other issues would quickly disabuse one of such a notion (see Rosen 1980). However, I wish to emphasize here the degree to which existing stations saw potential stations as a principal opponent.

TABLE 4.1.   Timeline of Radio Regulation, 1910–34

1910	First law governing radio communication, Wireless Ship Act of 1910, is passed; duties are assigned to the secretary of commerce and executed by the newly created Radio Service
1912	First law governing interstate radio is passed
1921	First commercial radio broadcast takes place; first commercial licenses are issued
1922	First paid radio advertisement is broadcast
1923	National Association of Broadcasters (NAB) is formed
1924	Network broadcasting begins
1927	Federal Radio Commission (FRC) is created by Congress in the Radio Act of 1927
1928	Davis Amendment mandates geographical distribution of radio stations
1930	Judicial review section of the 1927 act is amended (partially in response to the Supreme Court's *General Electric* ruling)
1934	Federal Communications Commission (FCC) is created by Congress in the Communications Act of 1934

the airwaves, is now in danger of becoming an anachronism. One report, for example, noted that the median AM station loses $11,000 each year.[2] Furthermore, nearly two hundred stations are currently unused—they are unprofitable and unable to attract new buyers.

Viewed through this lens, regulation of radio seems to be rather mundane compared to other areas of communications. It carries neither the flash and futuristic appeal of newer technologies nor the size and reach of television. Yet in the first few decades of the twentieth century, regulation of radio was the centerpiece of communications regulation. Before proceeding to an analysis of the Communications Act of 1934 and the judicial review provisions contained therein, it is useful to briefly outline the growth and importance of the industry in these earlier years, as summarized in table 4.1.[3] While this chapter provides a general overview of the development of the regulation of broadcasting, it does so while paying special attention to the role of interest groups.

Early Laws

The first federal law governing radio was the Wireless Ship Act of 1910. Reflecting the main use of radio at the time, this law merely mandated that all oceangoing vessels carrying fifty or more people be equipped with wireless equipment for contacting the shore. The U.S. secretary of commerce and labor was given responsibility for enforcing this act; the secretary in

---

    2. See Edmund L. Andrews, "F.C.C. Bid to revive AM Radio," *New York Times,* 27 September 1991.
    3. See also Coase's 1959 seminal survey and analysis of broadcasting regulation leading up to the 1934 act.

turn assigned the power to execute the act to the Bureau of Navigation's newly created Radio Service.[4]

Two years later Congress passed another law, this time regulating interstate (i.e., not just maritime) point-to-point radio. This bill required that every station be licensed, and it stipulated which frequencies were available for use.[5] Furthermore, it stipulated that whenever a station was in use, it had to be under the supervision of a person who had been properly licensed.

Under this new law, the U.S. Navy, which was the primary user of radio at the time, was accorded the best position on the spectrum, while amateurs were assigned to the outer edge of the spectrum (above 1500 kilohertz [kHz]). From the standpoint of later developments, the central feature of this act was that it provided a licensing scheme. This scheme, however, was essentially automatic; potential users simply had to register, and the secretary had little, if any, discretion regarding the awarding of licenses. At the time, the scheme worked satisfactorily, as amateurs and government users, such as the navy, were kept on separate parts of the radio band.

Over the next eight or nine years, there was very little change in the use of radio. Not even the pioneers of radio foresaw the explosion that was just over the horizon. The two major companies at the time were General Electric/RCA and Westinghouse, and the historical record suggests that rather than thinking of using radio for broadcasting, these corporate giants were instead occupied by selling phone calls and messages between private parties (Reck 1942). RCA admitted this lack of foresight in its 1922 annual report:

> At the time your corporation was formed in 1919, for the purpose of building up a world-wide international communication system, wireless telephone had not passed out of the experimental state, and it was not at that time foreseen that the broadcasting art would ever reach the high point of popularity that it has in the past year. The engineers and scientists had anticipated the development of wireless telephony for communication purposes, but no one had visualized the phenomenal expansion of wireless telephony as used today for broadcasting.[6]

RCA was not alone in lacking foresight. Congressional hearings held after World War I showed no mention of broadcasting, even by the president of

---

4. This act was amended on July 12, 1912, to include vessels sailing on the Great Lakes and to clarify that the fifty-person limit specified in the 1910 act included the crew.

5. Neither the 1910 nor the 1912 laws contained any provisions for judicial review.

6. Radio Corporation of America 1922, 18. Quoted in Severin 1978, 494.

the American Marconi company. Indeed, until the demonstrated success of some broadcasts in the early 1920s, most companies saw radio primarily as a means of point-to-point communication (Severin 1978, 493).

Beginning in the early 1920s, however, it was impossible *not* to notice the potential of commercial broadcasting, as the radio industry began to grow at an astonishing rate. The first commercial broadcasting license was issued to Pittsburgh station KDKA (owned by Westinghouse) in September 1921. In the next two months this station was joined by four other stations that received licenses. And then in December 1921 alone, 23 new station licenses were issued. This rapid increase represented just the beginning of the explosion. By the end of 1922, 576 stations were licensed, and the Department of Commerce estimated that between 600,000 and 1,000,000 people owned radios, compared to fewer than 50,000 one year earlier.[7]

This rapid rate of growth overwhelmed the simple licensing scheme created under the 1912 act and, more generally, threatened to undermine the development of radio. In response, Secretary of Commerce Herbert Hoover, with the cooperation of members of the radio industry, initiated a series of radio conferences, beginning in 1922, to deal with the growing problem of congestion. These conferences, which convened yearly, resulted in a number of legislative proposals. However, while there was nearly unanimous agreement that regulatory legislation was needed, there was sharp disagreement over *where* the regulatory power should be vested. The radio industry and many members of the House of Representatives wanted to give this power to Secretary Hoover's Department of Commerce, while the Senate argued for the creation of a new independent agency.

In 1927, spurred by court decisions that threatened to throw the industry into chaos, the different factions agreed on a compromise whereby an independent commission would be created for the period of one year, after which the Department of Commerce would take over most of its duties. At that time the commission would become an appellate body. The Radio Act of 1927 thereby created an independent commission,

---

7. The figures cited in this section come from J. Herring and Gross 1936, 244; Schmeckebier 1932, 4; and Minasian 1969, 401. While different sources give different estimates of the number of stations, the general trend is obvious. In addition to the implicit driving force of technology, another cause of this increase is the 1923 case of *Hoover v. Intercity Radio* (286 F. 1003), in which the District of Columbia Court of Appeals ruled that Congress had not delegated the authority to withhold licenses to the secretary of commerce in the Radio Act of 1912. *Hoover* "lowered the cost of entry by reducing the uncertainties created by the confusion about the discretionary power of the Secretary" (Minasian 1969, 401).

the Federal Radio Commission (FRC), to regulate—at least temporarily—the more than seven hundred stations in existence.[8]

The Federal Radio Commission

Interest in the work of the Federal Radio Commission—both public and private interest—was extremely high. In his contemporary evaluation of the early years of the FRC, Schmeckebier presents the following depiction of the situation:

> During the initial stages of the work of the Commission public interest in its work was probably more manifest than in the case of any regulatory activity ever undertaken by the government. Persons with decided views on prohibition, the tariff, or the regulation of railroads might grumble about the rulings, but comparatively few would take the time to write a letter. But if a broadcasting station appealed to its listeners for support, the mails were immediately clogged with thousands of letters. . . . (1932, 54)

In fact, in one instance more than 170,000 letters were submitted as evidence in a congressional hearing (E. Herring 1936, 165).

While general public interest was exceptionally high, so too was private interest. For one thing, radio provided an enormous opportunity for companies to advertise; in the early 1930s radio outpaced all other outlets in generating advertising money. In just the first half of 1932, three companies (American Tobacco, Standard Brands, and Pepsodent) spent nearly a million dollars on advertising at just one network (NBC), while several other companies also spent half a million dollars each at the same network (Rosen 1980, 159). In addition, prior to the arrival of advertising, most of the initial broadcast stations were owned by businesses that used their stations to advertise their wares and services.[9]

The groups with the strongest interest in the regulation of radio were those that wished to use the radio spectrum. Amateurs, educational and

---

8. Not surprisingly, this "temporary" arrangement was renewed each year by Congress, and eventually became permanent, as Senator Clarence Dill, a chief proponent of the compromise, later claims to have foreseen (Dill 1970). This chronology is discussed in more detail in chapter 6.

9. These businesses included electrical stores, department stores, music stores, garages, banks, theaters, newspapers, and, of course, radio manufacturers. But as we will see, as broadcasting became more expensive due to the costs of supplying and promoting programs, stations began to sell advertising time to a widening group of businesses. Soon most station owners were full-time radio people (J. Herring and Gross 1936, 103).

religious organizations, labor, other government agencies (such as the navy and the post office), and commercial broadcasters were involved at every step of the development of regulation from the 1910s through the 1930s because of their keen interest in the development of regulatory policy.[10] In part their interest was spurred by the opportunity to broadcast their views to the public; that was especially true for ideologically based groups. Ultimately, however, their interest was motivated by financial concerns. The monetary stakes involved were huge; in 1931, for example, broadcasters received over $77 million for rental of their facilities (E. Herring 1936, 170).[11]

Because of the huge financial opportunity presented by the radio industry, by far the most attentive of these groups were the commercial broadcasters. And this potential financial gain led, in the eyes of the FRC's early critics, to excessive interest-group influence:

> [T]he point seems clear that the Federal Radio Commission interpreted the concept of public interest so as to favor in actual practice one particular group. While talking in terms of the public interest, convenience, and necessity, the commission actually furthered the ends of the commercial broadcasters. (E. Herring 1936, 168)

While other histories of the FRC and FCC have not been so stridently critical, almost all have acknowledged the dominant role played by interest groups. Either by working directly with the agency or indirectly through members of Congress, these groups could bring pressure on the agency. And the pressure could be enormous.[12]

The National Association of Broadcasters

The main organization through which the commercial interests made their desires known was the National Association of Broadcasters (NAB).[13]

---

10. For example, see Hazlett's 1990 emphasis on the importance of different interest groups in developing a de facto, if not de jure, property rights scheme and McChesney's 1994 particularly lucid account of the battles between commercial broadcasters and radio reformers. See also the analysis by Coase (1959).

11. The broadcasting of views and opinions also should be considered a financial matter, as the use of radio drastically reduced the costs of penetrating homes.

12. One observer noted that "probably no quasi-judicial body was ever subjected to so much congressional pressure as the Federal Radio Commission" (Schmeckebier 1932, 54). Among the few authors who have downplayed the dominance of commercial broadcasters and the captured nature of the FRC are Douglas (1987, 97) and Stone (1991, 11).

13. There were, of course, other organizations, but the NAB was by far the most important for commercial broadcasters. Llewellyn White pithily describes the imbalance: "To be

Formed in 1923, this organization came together as a result of the radio conferences organized by Secretary of Commerce Herbert Hoover and was the main force agitating for federal regulation in the 1920s. Although it seemingly lost a major battle over the creation of an independent radio commission, it quickly recovered and, due to both the temporary nature of the Radio Commission and the commission's location outside the executive branch, found that it was able to exert far greater influence on this commission than it would have been able to on the Department of Commerce. The following passage illustrates the depth of the NAB's interests and its ability to push its agenda, which included, among other things, *keeping its licenses* and *preventing new stations from being created:*

> That agenda focused on "the non-issuance of additional broadcasting licenses, the freedom from further division of time with other broadcasters, [and] the maintenance of the present distribution of frequency channels," as the 1925 Radio Conference's resolution . . . put it. In the months preceding the February 23, 1927, passage of the Radio Act, this strategy was quite clear, and its influence in shaping the Act was understood by informed observers both within and without the industry. As Morris Ernst wrote, "the proposed legislation contains phrases such as 'public utility,' 'public necessity,' and 'public interest,' but the operation of the bill is for private profit and for the stabilization of investment."
>
> This agenda was artfully accomplished. When the Federal Radio Commission (FRC) was born out of the Federal Radio Act of 1927, it immediately grandfathered rights for major broadcasters, while eliminating marginal competitors and all new entry. (Hazlett 1990, 154; footnotes omitted)

This analysis is borne out by a careful reading of the *Broadcasters' News Bulletin* (and later the *NAB Reports*), the trade journal of broadcasters.[14] Time and again during the 1920s and early 1930s, these reports issued calls to arms for existing stations to join together to protect themselves against the potential incursions of newcomers. The following passage is representative of the viewpoint expressed in these reports:

> Broadcasting is the most regulated business in the world. . . . Interests that have stood passively by and were unwilling to bear the trials of

---

sure, NAB is not the only radio association. Some of the others are worth noting, if only to observe how little impact they have had on the medium as a whole" (1947, 85).

14. These newsletters can be found in archives at the headquarters of the National Association of Broadcasters in Washington, D.C.

pioneering are now endeavoring to *invade the broadcast band at the expense of existing stations.* While broadcasters throughout the United States are busily engaged at home performing the exacting duty of developing programs for the public, those who are designedly seeking to enter the broadcasting field are effectively organized in Washington. . . . Broadcasters must unite or they cannot withstand the impending onslaughts. Broadcasters must organize for self-preservation. (*Broadcasters' News Bulletin,* n.d. [1931]; emphasis added)

This refrain was quite common in these reports. The NAB constantly was arguing in newsletters and special bulletins that existing stations needed to band together to protect their interests; and the rivals that broadcasters most needed protection against were potential entrants.

Other Groups

What countervailing forces existed to combat the strong pressure from the radio interests? Other interests can be grouped loosely into two main constituencies—nonprofit broadcasters and listeners' associations.[15] Despite the weakness of these groups relative to the radio interests, they were able to achieve some successes. For example, when the House and Senate were battling over the final form of the 1927 act, a group representing educational broadcasters was able to persuade Senator Dill (D-WA) to include special protection for educational broadcasters from incursions by commercial stations, a provision that ultimately was included in the law. Still, reflecting their general inability to coalesce and exert influence, these countervailing forces were almost completely unsuccessful in obtaining desired substantive outcomes, in affecting the drafting of the law, or even in raising concerns that commercial broadcasters were dominating the process (Hazlett 1990; McChesney 1994).

Moving into the 1930s

Most of the foregoing discussion relies on accounts of the political situation during the 1920s and the battles fought at that time in setting up the

---

15. As Hazlett (1990) and also Rosen (1980) nicely detail, self-interested bureaucrats comprised another "interest group." This group was mostly important in the 1910s, when turf wars were being fought between the navy, the Department of Commerce, and the post office. Others opposed to commercial broadcasting included labor, the ACLU, and intellectuals. An example of the latter is pointedly captured in H. L. Mencken's characterization of commercial broadcasting as "an almost unbroken series of propaganda harangues by quacks with something to sell, and of idiotic comments upon public events by persons devoid of both information and ideas" (quoted in McChesney 1994, 95).

original regulatory scheme. When debate began over what would become the Communications Act of 1934, several years of regulation by a generally sympathetic agency had increased the power of the commercial interests relative to their competitors.[16] The reformers more actively tried to affect the regulatory law, but they were hardly more successful.

The Decline of Noncommercial Stations

The most unmistakable change during this time was the increase in the power of commercial interests and the concomitant decline in the power of the noncommercial interests. In the early and mid-1920s, noncommercial broadcasters saw their numbers proliferate, only to see them recede in the late 1920s and early 1930s. For example, the number of college stations peaked at 128 in 1925, then dropped by nearly two-thirds over the next five years. Of the more than 200 educational licenses granted in the 1920s and early 1930s, by 1936 only 38 remained.[17] This decline of noncommercial broadcasting was duly noted during congressional hearings by Senator Wagner, who observed that by 1934 noncommercial broadcasters accounted for less than 2 percent of all broadcast time: "I hold no brief against the commercial stations, but I do not believe they are entitled to 98 percent of the time."[18]

What accounts for this decline in fortunes? In part, it was due to the lack of support and funding from educational institutions (J. Herring and Gross 1936, 428). But the strategic actions of the commercial broadcasters and the government also played a role. An advocate of educational radio described the situation in the 1930s as follows:

> The practice of squeezing these stations off the air ran something like this. First, they would be given the less desirable frequencies, the more desirable being assigned to the commercial and monopoly groups. Second, they would be required to divide their time with some

---

16. Nongovernmental groups represented during hearings on S. 2910 and H.R. 8301, the forerunners of the Communications Act, included the following: radio businesses (the NAB, RCA, Pacific-Western Broadcasting Federation); religious organizations (the Organization of Catholic Priests, the Watchtower Bible and Tract Society); labor (the American Federation of Labor, Electrical Workers Union); and various telephone and telegraph companies and groups.

17. See Severin 1978, McChesney 1994, and Smulyan 1994. Another measure of the decline of noncommercial broadcasters is that by 1934, about two-thirds of all broadcasting stations belonged to the NAB. Equally revealing is Smulyan's disclosure that between 1921 and 1926, 177 new educational licenses were issued while 94 were lost; but between 1927 and 1931, only 12 new educational licenses were issued while 64 were lost.

18. See Senate consideration of S. 3285 from May 15, 1934 (*Cong. Rec.,* 73d Cong., 2d sess., 1934, 78, pt. 8:8831).

commercial interest. Third, they would be required to give a larger share of their time to commercial interest [*sic*]. Fourth, they would be required to meet some new regulation involving costly equipment— often a regulation essentially right in itself but applied with such suddenness as not to allow time for adjustment in the educational budget. Fifth, the educational station would be required to spend, on trips to Washington for hearings before the Federal Radio Commission and lawyer's fees, the money which should have gone into the development of personnel and programs.[19]

As this passage makes clear, the FRC was not an innocent bystander in the demise of noncommercial stations, but rather was seen by nonprofit broadcasters as complicit. Despite FRC claims to the contrary, many nonprofits blamed the commission for their demise:

> The Commission may boast that it has never cut an educational station off the air. It merely cuts off our head, our arms, and our legs, and then allows us to die a natural death. (Quoted in McChesney 1994, 31)

And many actions by the FRC, such as the issuance of General Order 40, which reallocated stations in a manner extremely favorable to large commercial stations, supported this impression of the FRC.[20]

One agency action in particular hurt many noncommercial stations and sent a warning signal to others. When the FRC was created, it saw one of its primary tasks as reducing the congestion on the air. By 1928 it had made little headway toward accomplishing this goal, and so on May 25, 1928, it issued General Order 32, which notified 164 stations that they were to appear before the commission "to make a showing that their continued operation would serve public interest, convenience, and necessity" (Federal Radio Commission 1928, 15).[21] This defense of their licenses involved coming to Washington for a hearing. Not surprisingly, more than half the stations singled out in this manner were substantially affected. Altogether, 81 did manage to escape adverse action, but 12 others were given reduced

---

19. This passage, quoted in Severin 1978, 497, is from Joy E. Morgan's "National Committee on Education by Radio," *Education by Radio* 1, no. 20 (June 25, 1931): 79.

20. This order, issued in August 1928, altered the frequency assignments of 94 percent of stations, sparing only large and chain-owned stations (McChesney 1994, 25).

21. Among the stations forced off the air by such tactics were Nebraska Wesleyan and Carleton College of Northfield, Minnesota: "Because of long and expensive litigation to remain on the air, Carleton allowed its broadcast license to expire on April 1, 1933. . . ." (Severin 1978, 499).

hours, 4 received probation, 5 were forced to consolidate with other stations, and the remainder were taken off the air. Because of the expense involved, nearly one-third of the stations never even appeared for the hearings (Federal Radio Commission 1928).[22]

One final episode illustrates the growing power of commercial stations vis-à-vis noncommercial stations. In the days leading up to the passage of the Communications Act of 1934, several members of Congress pushed for an amendment to guarantee that a portion of the spectrum be reserved for educational and other noncommercial stations. This amendment was defeated in the Senate, and in its place the FCC was directed to study the desirability of such an action. To the dismay of the educational stations, but to the surprise of few close observers, the FCC reported that under the existing arrangement, in which educational stations were given no special status, the public interest was being served. Commercial stations, asserted the FCC, already were doing a suitable job of serving the public interest by allocating large portions of their on-air time to educational purposes.

The predominance of commercial broadcasters, by the time Congress began deliberations about creating a communications commission in the 1930s, thus was even greater than it had been in the 1920s. The main change between the mid-1920s and the early 1930s was simply that the power of commercial interests had expanded while at the same time the power of the noncommercial interests had declined.[23]

Changes within the Commercial Broadcasting Industry

As the previous section demonstrates, the gap in power between the commercial and noncommercial stations grew larger in the period between 1927 and 1934. Within the commercial broadcasting industry, two noteworthy new features appeared at this time, features that occurred concurrently but separately and soon became intertwined.[24] The first of these was the growth in importance of advertising as a source of revenue; the second was the development of the network system of broadcasting.[25] In dis-

---

22. As a University of Illinois station director complained, "we practically wasted all of the money that the university has put into our broadcasting efforts" in hearings before the FRC (McChesney 1994, 31).

23. As McChesney has observed, "it would be difficult to exaggerate the harmonious and extensive relationship that had developed between the FRC on the one hand and NBC, CBS, and the NAB on the other hand. This relationship is all the more striking given the near total lack of contact the FRC had with nonprofit broadcasters . . ." (1994, 23).

24. Much of the remainder of this chapter draws on Head 1976, Barnouw 1966, and Inglis 1990, as well J. Herring and Gross 1936, Smulyan 1994, and McChesney 1994.

25. The single best analysis of the growth of advertising is Smulyan 1994.

cussing these changes, I will continue to advance the argument that the goals of the commercial broadcasters during this time increasingly became keeping their own licenses and limiting entry for others.

The Growth of Advertising

In the initial days of broadcasting, as indicated earlier, one of the primary incentives for companies to engage in broadcasting was to advertise their own goods or services. At the forefront of this movement were the manufacturers of radio receivers. As early as 1920, Westinghouse saw the potential for this symbiotic relationship between manufacturing radio sets and broadcasting.[26] It saw that it could manufacture inexpensive receivers and then create a market for them by broadcasting programs over the airwaves. In other words, broadcasting would be used to stimulate demand for newly manufactured receivers.

This use of radio for purposes of self-advertisement was one of the primary incentives for many of the early broadcasters. Many businesses, such as hardware stores and newspapers, broadcast entertainment and news programs simply to attract attention to their goods and services.[27] Others, like Westinghouse, did so in order to create a market for their products.[28]

It soon became apparent that there were two dominant groups within the ranks of broadcasters, and these two groups had different philosophies about radio. One of these groups, known as the Radio Group, shared the same goals as Westinghouse. This group, which included General Electric and RCA in addition to Westinghouse,

> started with the idea of operating broadcast stations as a means of stimulating the market for their consumer goods. Therefore, their broadcast stations assumed responsibility for supplying both the physical facilities and the messages sent over these facilities. . . . The Radio Group emphasized the public's interest in receiving a program service—at the price of investment in receiving equipment. According to this approach, any firm that wanted to use broadcasting to create

---

26. The company found itself uniquely situated to undertake this entrepreneurial effort because of its devotion to and investment in the production of radio equipment for the military during World War I (Leblebici et al. 1991).

27. A 1926 survey revealed that about half of all stations were operated to draw attention to the parent company's products. See McChesney 1994,15.

28. Westinghouse was more than willing to bear all the costs of broadcasting, and in fact did not even want outside advertisers, because of the favorable publicity the company was receiving for its broadcasts over KDKA (Head 1976, 111). As RCA's David Sarnoff commented, "we broadcast primarily so that those who purchase [RCA radios] may have something to feed those receiving instruments with" (Smulyan 1994, 37).

public good will for its products would operate its own separate station for that purpose. (Head 1976, 115)

The other group, known as the Telephone Group, was dominated by AT&T. Not surprisingly, this group saw radio as a variant of the telephone. This group's vision of the future of radio included a limited number of stations that would be available to others for use in broadcasting messages.

Eventually, members of the Telephone Group dropped out of broadcasting. But their conception of radio, in which people would hire radio stations and use their transmitters to broadcast messages to a large audience, was a harbinger of the future. The first paid advertisement took place on August 28, 1922, over WEAF, which was AT&T's flagship station. On this date, WEAF, for a price of $50, allowed a real estate developer to promote the Hawthorne Courts apartment complex in New York. Thus began the age of advertising over the radio.

The idea of using radio for advertising soon caught on. While over the next few years many stations continued to be operated by their owners for self-promotion only, by 1930 this use of radio had been overtaken by the use of radio as a means of generating revenue from advertisers. And this revenue, rather than the benefits received from either promoting one's own business or creating a market for receivers, became the primary means of financial support for commercial broadcasters.[29]

Evidence of this change is provided by contemporary discussions of the for-profit nature of the radio industry. While the importance in the early and mid-1920s of broadcasting as a means by which to stimulate the demand for receivers was apparent, by the 1930s the situation had changed and advertising was seen as the key:

> During the early days of broadcasting, little attention was paid to the costs of broadcasting. Those who owned and operated stations had products and services of their own to exploit. While the novelty lasted, almost any kind of program satisfied the listeners, kilocycle or station hunting presenting in itself sufficient sport, and the marketers of radio receiving apparatus reaped a harvest. So did the marketers of

---

29. The use of advertising was far from unanimously embraced. Early on, for example, RCA's David Sarnoff ridiculed and criticized the idea. Broadcasters remained on the defensive about advertising for years; even in the 1930s, many of the editorial opinions in the *NAB Reports* continued to be dedicated to a defense of the use of advertising over the air. To minimize criticism, the industry was careful to adhere to a strict set of self-imposed regulations regarding advertising, including rules that allowed advertising during business hours only and that prohibited the mentioning of prices.

broadcasting equipment with the flood of new stations. But the situation soon changed. The demands of listeners became more exacting as the novelty wore off, talent began to demand more than publicity for their services, and many of the stations found broadcasting too expensive. The result was inevitable. A number of stations ceased broadcasting altogether, while others sold their equipment to those interested in broadcasting exclusively, not as a hobby. (J. Herring and Gross 1936, 102–3)

By the late 1920s, therefore, the primary financial incentive for those who wished to profit from radio broadcasting clearly lay in the collection of revenues from advertising. And as seen in table 4.2, the revenues from advertising increased dramatically and continuously at this time.

The Birth of the Network System

The second important change within the industry at this time was the development of the network system.[30] Initially, few people (with the exception of visionaries like David Sarnoff) had given much thought to the idea of broadcasting over a network of stations. Once started, however, networks quickly caught on, creating a new world within the broadcasting industry.

Not only did AT&T occupy a central place in the development of radio as a medium for advertisement, it also was the originator of the network system of broadcasting. Early in 1923, AT&T experimented with the idea of network broadcasting, using its phone lines to transmit broadcast

TABLE 4.2.   Advertising Revenues (millions of dollars)

Year	All Stations	NBC and CBS
1927	$4.8	3.8
1928	14.1	10.3
1929	26.8	18.7
1930	40.5	26.8
1931	56.0	35.8
1932	61.9	39.2
1933	57.0	31.7
1934	72.8	42.7

Sources: Broadcasting Yearbook 1939; Sterling and Kittross 1990; J. Herring and Gross 1936.

30. The two principal characteristics of network systems are "(1) two or more stations connected together; and (2) simultaneous broadcasting of the *same* program" (T. Robinson 1943, 34).

material from one station to another.[31] By later that year, AT&T had in place the nation's first permanent radio network. And by 1924, AT&T had in place a network system that supplied stations in cities along the East Coast with several hours of programming each day.

Although it initially lacked access to AT&T's phone lines, the Radio Group was not far behind in experimenting with a network system.[32] Then, when AT&T decided to get out of the radio business, the Radio Group quickly bought AT&T's stations and its network system. This system, with WEAF as its flagship station, soon became known as the Red Network, and a second network—the Blue Network, with station WJZ at its center—was formed shortly thereafter.[33] And in 1927, the United Independent Broadcasters (later the Columbia Broadcast System, or CBS) formed a competing national network.

By the late 1920s, the network system already had become the dominant feature of national radio broadcasting. By 1928, roughly 40 percent of the stations in operation had become network affiliates. And this number, while impressive, actually understates the power of the networks, as most of the unaffiliated stations were low-watt stations.[34] In addition, some 98 percent of the nighttime broadcasts were over network affiliates (Head 1976, 140).

Networks and Advertising

The simultaneity of the development of the network system and the growth of advertising was not a chance occurrence. Prospective advertisers saw the opportunities inherent in radio, especially the promise of advertising over a network, and began approaching AT&T even before WEAF first went on the air. The attraction for both sides was clear. Advertising revenues provided the financial means for networks to continue to develop, and at the same time, networks gave advertisers access to a much wider market. The size of advertising revenues clearly reflected the

---

31. The program originated at WEAF in New York and was transmitted over the telephone lines to WNAC in Boston.

32. The Radio Group, denied access to AT&T's far superior telephone lines, initially was forced to transmit over Western Union's less adaptable telegraph lines.

33. By this time the Radio Group had formed NBC (the National Broadcasting Company) as a wholly owned subsidiary. WEAF later became WNBC. WJZ eventually became WABC and then later became WCBS when the station was purchased by CBS in 1928. The Blue Network, sans WJZ, was sold in 1945 and became ABC.

34. An FRC survey on commercial radio advertising for the period November 8 to 14, 1931, reported that only two of the forty clear channels in existence were not used by chains (J. Herring and Gross 1936, 101).

growing national market and the close ties between national networks and advertising (again see table 4.2).

The Goals of Commercial Broadcasters

The world of commercial broadcasting had clearly undergone striking changes during the 1920s. Both the advent of the network system and the growth of advertising led to many changes in the industry and its environment. But despite these changes, it remains clear that the dominant forces within the industry shared the twin goals of keeping their licenses and limiting entry.[35] Although it could be argued to the contrary, it was not the case that these forces sought to allow expanded entry. To see why that was so, let us first examine and then refute potential reasons for preferring expanded entry.

First, one might argue that interference, while still existent, was less of a problem than it had been. There is certainly some truth to this assertion. In the first few years of its existence, the FRC had set out to accomplish several main goals, including reducing interference, allocating licenses in an equitable fashion, and engaging in such activities while comporting with its mandate to act in the public interest.

Although it was subject to a great deal of criticism, the FRC did make some progress toward accomplishing these goals. In just a few short years, it was able to produce a strongly defensible record and some ardent supporters:

> No one who recalls the chaotic broadcasting situation which prevailed at the time when the Commission took office can fail to appreciate the significance of its work in reducing interference and in raising technical standards for transmitting apparatus and station operation. (J. Herring and Gross 1936, 426)

Yet while the agency did a commendable job, it was still the case that after several years of work there were too many stations on the air. Throughout the period from 1927 to 1934, the number of stations on the air remained roughly constant. In effect, however, because the average power of stations had increased during this time, the agency's failure to *reduce* the number of stations actually exacerbated the amount of interference (Eoyang 1936).

---

35. Again, this observation is not meant to imply that broadcasters were a monolithic force on every issue. But when it was in their interest to band together, they did.

Despite their best efforts, then, the FRC failed to lessen the number of stations on the air, and therefore was not able to eliminate the problem of interference. Even supporters of the commission were forced to admit that there were still too many stations on the air.[36] Part of the problem was that in trying to eliminate stations that had been broadcasting for years, the FRC found itself faced with lengthy court battles and angry members of Congress. These hurdles made largely unsuccessful its attempts to solve such problems on a case-by-case basis (Krasnow, Longley, and Terry, 1982). And even when it attempted to use a "show cause" order to remove many of the weaker stations, nearly half were able to stay on the air. Accordingly, it can be argued that the agency

> failed to take effective action on the most pressing problem—the need to sharply reduce the number of stations in operation. The commission chipped away at this problem over a number of years. From 1927 to 1932 it reduced the total number of broadcast authorizations, but only from 681 to 604. (Head 1976, 132)[37]

Even given that the Radio Commission was unable to substantially reduce the number of stations, and thereby eliminate interference, was it the case that the commercial stations preferred lowered barriers to entry anyway? One potential reason station owners might prefer lowered entry barriers would be to increase the sales of receivers, which would parallel Westinghouse's logic in the early 1920s. That is, many of the large stations that were engaged in the manufacturing of receivers, including Westinghouse and RCA, the two principal owners of NBC, wanted more stations in order to stimulate the demand for radio sets.

As we have seen, however, by the 1930s, revenues from advertising were far and away the primary financial motivation for commercial broadcasters. While a few station owners, such as RCA, obviously stood to benefit from sales of receivers, accounts of the profitability of owning sta-

---

36. See especially J. Herring and Gross 1936, 254. It should be noted that these authors argue that congestion remained a problem only in certain (unspecified) parts of the country. And they repeatedly emphasize that the agency did a tremendous job of reducing, if not eliminating, the problems of interference.

37. Again, it was widely acknowledged that there were too many stations. Louis Caldwell, a lifelong participant in the radio industry who served as the General Counsel for the FRC, wrote: "On one matter there is, apparently, universal agreement: there are far too many broadcasting stations. . . . The decrease from 732 to 608 has been more apparent than real, since the eliminations have been largely of small stations in the local class which are not very troublesome factors in the problem, and there have been many increases of power among stations of the regional class, which cause the greatest difficulty" (1930, 117–18).

tions at that time do not even mention such sales as a source of income when discussing the financial incentives of station owners.[38] In any case, radio manufacturers would be able to sell the most sets when there was clear reception. Promoting increased numbers of stations at the expense of clear reception would clearly be counterproductive.[39]

Another potential reason for preferring eased entry, one that is related to the reason given earlier, would be to start new stations. Networks and commercial stations, after all, could reap greater benefits from advertisers if they could claim to reach a larger and broader audience. And while congestion was a problem in the bigger cities, it was much less of a problem in rural areas. Hence, the station owners might seek to stimulate demand by giving citizens who currently could not receive any signals access to new stations.

This argument that the station owners were looking to start new stations, however, neglects that the fact that by the 1930s the entire country was able to enjoy reception of radio broadcasts. Two factors were especially pivotal in establishing this situation. First, the Davis Amendment, passed in 1928, had forced the FRC to allocate stations equally across five geographical zones, and within those zones by population. This amendment provided at least the minimal guarantee that stations would be widely, and hopefully fairly, scattered.

Second, the development of clear-channel stations, again in the 1920s, had been set up to help ensure service to rural areas. When the Radio Commission was created in 1927, it was able to reduce urban congestion by reallocating stations' broadcast frequencies. It did so by maintaining, as far as possible, 50 kHz separations between stations operating in the same area. Such separations, however, did little to alleviate interference in rural areas, which often would receive signals from two stations that were located in different areas but that were required to broadcast on the same frequency.

---

38. For example, Thomas Porter Robinson, in his history of the radio networks, identifies advertising as "the fairy godmother of the broadcasting business," (1943, 13) but makes no mention of the desire to sell sets after the first few years of the 1920s.

39. I do not want to minimize the importance to some companies of selling radios. These sales accounted for huge revenues for manufacturers—in millions of dollars, the total annual sales for the years 1925 through 1928 were $430, $506, $426, and $651, respectively (*Broadcasting Yearbook* 1939). RCA alone was selling $50 million in sets per year by 1924 (T. Robinson 1943). And at the end of 1934, only 65 percent of households had radio receivers (Eoyang 1936), indicating the continued existence of a large, untapped market. The point is, as I will continue to argue, that stations were already transmitting into all areas of the country, and listeners could hear them. Finally, it should be noted that by this time, most purchases were of better sets, not new sets (e.g., ones operated on alternating current rather than batteries).

To address this problem, in the fall of 1927 the commission designated the band of stations from 600 to 1000 kHz as "clear-channel" stations. Essentially, this designation meant that only one station *anywhere* could broadcast at the given frequency. Especially at night, such a system provided rural listeners with access to radio stations.[40] And, as might be expected, these clear-channel stations were by and large affiliated with the networks, thus providing them—and those who advertised on their stations—with access to rural listeners. Congestion was certainly less of a problem in rural areas, but one cannot extrapolate from that to the idea that networks and larger stations wanted more new stations in these areas. Adding more stations in these areas would not have increased their advertising markets because given the reach of the network system—and especially the clear-channel set-up—the networks were already reaching most areas of the country. And new stations might have interfered with the existing signals.

One final point that should be made is that the networks and other large station owners clearly did want to expand into markets where they did not already own stations. This desire alone might make it seem that these powerful stations would prefer easier entry. But once again, the situation was not so simple. In fact, when larger companies such as RCA moved into new territories, they generally did so not by starting up *new* stations, but rather by buying *existing* stations. With stations constantly failing for financial and other reasons, these corporate giants looking to expand had less of an incentive to start up new stations.

Such had been the case since the days of Department of Commerce regulation. In hearings before Congress, a representative for the department allowed that the license was seen as attaching to the apparatus, and not the person. This perspective implied that when a license could not be obtained by application, it could be obtained by purchase. This practice continued under the Radio Commission, providing a way for existing stations to expand their empires without having to create new stations from the ground up (Barnouw 1966, 174).[41]

---

40. The clear-channel system was somewhat more complicated than this basic description. There were two classes of clear channels. One set of stations, which might be called "completely clear," had exclusive use of their channels. Another set had a somewhat less privileged position, and each shared its frequency with another station. The other station, however, was usually small, distant, and operated only during the daytime.

41. Here was yet another tactic by which commercial stations sought to overpower noncommercial stations. When both shared a channel assignment, commercial stations often would petition the FRC for full-time use of the station. The commission would then set up hearings on the matter, but because these hearings often were lengthy and too expensive for the noncommercial stations, they would often just give up. Such actions occurred twenty-eight times in 1931 alone (Barnouw 1966, 261).

The goal of reducing interference consequently remained predominant for most commercial stations. While there were some advantages to having more stations, especially in certain parts of the country, these advantages tended to be outweighed by the disadvantages. Even as late as the 1960s, one of the primary goals of the FCC remained providing existing stations with freedom from interference. And in the 1930s, such was unequivocally the case. Reduction of interference, which could in part be accomplished by making it more difficult for potential stations to get licenses, continued to be a primary goal of most commercial broadcasters.

Changes in Technology

In order to think about the changes in the industry between 1927 and 1934, a final factor that needs to be explored is whether technology changed dramatically during this period. One answer to this question is that technology obviously improved continuously during that time. In fact, the story of the first fifteen years or so of commercial broadcasting can be told as one of continual technological innovation. Throughout that time, for example, radios became better at receiving signals without interference and transmitters became stronger. Stricter engineering standards were enforced, taking advantage of technological improvements to ensure, for example, that stations became better at broadcasting directly on their own wavelength and did not wander around the spectrum. There is little doubt that improved technology helped decrease interference.

Still, it is equally clear from the previous section that these technological developments alone were not enough to eliminate the twin problems of congestion and interference. In addition, broadcasters were not able to take advantage of all the technological improvements. For example, despite the improved ability of stations to send out a constant signal on a given wavelength, the 10 kHz channel spacing standard, used since the early days of Department of Commerce regulation, continued to be enforced.[42]

More important, some of the major technological breakthroughs that substantially contributed to the reduction of interference, such as the invention of the directional antenna, did not occur until later.[43] Thus, while technological improvements in radio broadcasting clearly helped reduce congestion and interference, some of the major developments in this regard did not arrive until after the passage of the Communications Act of 1934, and those that predated this act were not enough, on their own, to eliminate these problems.

---

42. Indeed, in 1939, the FCC's *Standards of Good Engineering Practice* formalized this de facto standard (Inglis 1990).

43. The directional antenna, which was developed in the mid-1930s by RCA, had a profound impact in reducing interference and improving reception quality (Inglis 1990, 58).

CHAPTER 5

Interest Groups, Judicial Review, and Broadcast Regulation

Even though only a very small proportion of the FCC's actions are reviewed by the courts, the significance of judicial review in the commission's policy-making cannot be measured by statistical analysis alone. Judicial review, no matter how seldom invoked, hangs as a threatening possibility over each administrative or legislative decision. (Krasnow, Longley, and Terry 1982, 62)

The previous chapter has given us a better understanding of the nature of interest-group influence over the regulation of radio, and of the goals and incentives of these groups. In this chapter I will examine the actions of the groups, in light of the arguments and theoretical ideas developed earlier, to explain the design of judicial review of broadcasting policy and the 1934 Communications Act.

To understand the Communications Act of 1934, much less any specific provisions within the act, one must first look back to 1927, the year the Federal Radio Commission was created. The reasons for this look into the past are clear—while the Federal Communications Commission was technically a new agency, in reality its responsibilities were constructed by combining the regulation of common carriers previously vested in the Interstate Commerce Commission with the existing jurisdiction of the Federal Radio Commission. Thus, in this chapter I will examine both the 1927 and 1934 acts, with a special emphasis on the role of interest groups.

Judicial Review under the Radio Act of 1927

Guidelines for judicial review were set forth in Section 16 of the Radio Act of 1927 (see appendix B). There were five main facets of review specified in this section, dealing with the reviewability of agency actions, standing, the scope of review, the time frame in which an appeal had to be made, and the designation of which courts were responsible for review. To begin with, Section 16 provided for appeals from both *refusals* and *revocations*—

refusals of applications (for construction permits, licenses, license renewals, and license modifications) and revocations of licenses. According to Cass, the 1927 law provided for review of only this small set of decisions because

> The initial structure of the Radio Act made broad prescription of judicial review unnecessary: the FRC was to serve as an adjudicatory, appellate body, not one exercising sweeping administrative powers, and judicial review could logically be confined to those decisions the FRC was expected to make. (1989, 82)[1]

This limited reviewability soon created some problems. Since only refusals and revocations were appealable, many station owners feared that the FRC would have too much power to alter unilaterally the terms of a station's license while also plausibly claiming that it had not denied the license. And in several cases, the FRC did just that, claiming that it had granted an application, albeit on terms different from what was sought by the licensee. In other words, what constituted a denial was ambiguous. However, the District of Columbia Court of Appeals ultimately disagreed with the FRC's approach, holding that such actions could be appealed.[2]

The second notable feature of the review provisions dealt with the issue of who had standing to seek redress from the courts. According to the legislation, only the applicant or licensee whose application was denied or whose license was revoked had the right to appeal, even though the modification of a license might have affected many other parties. For example, an existing station might suffer interference due to the issuance of a license to a new station on the same frequency.[3] The existing station,

---

1. This argument derives from the circumstances surrounding the creation of the FRC. As noted in the previous chapter, the commission originally was created to exercise administrative authority over radio licensing for one year only, after which time the Department of Commerce was supposed to take over the duties as the licensing authority.

2. This matter was addressed in the *General Electric* case discussed later in this chapter. Of that decision, Caldwell wrote that "an application for a permit (or license, or renewal of license, or modification of license) having certain terms and conditions is not to be considered granted by the issuance of an instrument having terms and conditions other than those applied for. This is clear from the decision in the *General Electric* case, where a renewal license authorized reduced hours of operation, and from a dictum in *White v. FRC* (29 F.2d 113), where a renewal license authorized reduced power" (1930, 283).

3. That was common practice in the early years of broadcasting. In fact, initially *all* broadcast stations, with the exception of those dealing with crop and weather forecasts, were assigned to the same frequency—833 kHz—and had to work out informal arrangements, such as broadcasting at different times of the day, in order for their signals to be heard without interference. In 1922, in an attempt to ease congestion, the Radio Conference, led by Secretary of Commerce Hoover, added a second (and more prestigious and powerful) frequency

in this case, would not have had the right to appeal. In effect, this provision meant that standing in cases involving disputes over radio licenses was limited.

Third, the statute specified the scope of review. While the number of issues over which the courts had jurisdiction (i.e., reviewability) was limited, the provisions of Section 16 gave the courts wide latitude in reaching a decision on those issues. Rather than simply being restricted to questions of law, the courts were given the power to review de novo the actions of the commission.[4]

Viewed in this light, the statute's grant of judicial review was quite broad, especially in comparison with the provisions for review of other existing agencies.[5] Cushman (1941) explains that this breadth was due to the scope of powers given to the Radio Commission:

> It was widely felt that the power to grant, revoke, or modify station licenses, a power to be exercised under the vague guiding standard of the public interest, convenience, and necessity, was too vitally important to be exercised by any administrative body without judicial review of the most complete scope. Accordingly, the Court of Appeals of the District of Columbia was authorized to review the decisions of the proposed radio commission in license matters and to reach its own independent judgement regarding the soundness and justice of the commission's action. (Cushman 1941, 308–9)

While the set of decisions therefore was confined, within that set the courts were given sweeping powers.

---

at 750 kHz. Of course, even that was not enough, and in the following year the conference decided to allocate commercial broadcasting the range from 550 kHz to 1350 kHz (expanded to 1500 kHz in 1924).

4. Section 16 stipulates that "either party may give notice to the court of his desire to adduce additional evidence" and that "the court shall hear, review, and determine the appeal upon said record and evidence, and may alter or revise the decision appealed from and enter such judgement as to it may seem just." For more analysis of this point, see Cass 1989, 82.

5. When the Federal Trade Commission (FTC) was created in 1914, for example, there was considerable debate over whether the courts should be constrained by the commission's findings of fact. The legislation ultimately stipulated that "the findings of the commission as to the facts, if supported by testimony, [are] conclusive." Furthermore, the court was limited to the record as generated by the commission's investigation. See McFarland 1933, 43; and Cushman 1941,201–4. Interestingly, one of the primary proponents of narrow judicial review of FTC actions—in particular, that the courts should defer to agency expertise—was Senator Albert Cummins, who later became one of the key players in the development of radio regulation during the 1920s. Consistent with his preference for limited review, he argued that the allowance of de novo review of the FRC by the courts was constitutionally invalid (*Cong. Rec.* 69th Cong., 1st sess., 1926, 67, pt. 11:12354; see also Cushman 1941, 309, 313).

The final two provisions deserving of mention deal with the time frame in which an agency action could be reviewed and the courts to which appeals could be taken. Concerning the time frame, appellants were given the relatively short period of twenty days to file an appeal. And regarding the location of review, while all qualified participants (as defined by the clause dealing with standing) were allowed to appeal to the Court of Appeals of the District of Columbia, a licensee who suffered a revocation also had the option of appealing such an action to the local United States district court.[6]

The Supreme Court Intervenes

This mode of judicial review provisions did not last long, however. On May 19, 1930, the Supreme Court, in *Federal Radio Commission v. General Electric Company*,[7] effectively undercut some of the provisions of Section 16.

The *General Electric* case arose because of controversies over the license renewal of Schenectady station WGY, owned by the General Electric Company. Since 1923, WGY had operated on the 790-kilocycle frequency, sharing time amicably with a second station, WHAZ. But in 1928 the FRC ruled that WGY would have to share the frequency with another station, San Francisco's KGO, and furthermore could not operate after sunset. WGY appealed the commission's decision, and the District of Columbia court reversed and remanded the case to the commission.

Upon appeal, the Supreme Court refused to hear the case. In making this decision, Justice Van Devanter argued that when the Court of Appeals reviewed agency decisions de novo, it was acting in an *administrative* capacity. But, according to Van Devanter, the Supreme Court, as an Article III constitutional court, could review only *judicial* findings. Therefore, appeals from lower court decisions could not be taken to the Supreme Court.

This decision has not been heralded as a shining light of legal reasoning. At the time, Louis Caldwell (1930, 277) openly but kindly questioned the decision, observing, "The opinion of the Supreme Court is not as clear as might be desired. . . ." before launching into a dissection of Van

---

6. Two additional comments should be made. First, note that this provision allowed only those who already owned a station to appeal to the local district court. Second, of 118 cases appealed to the courts between 1927 and 1932, only three were appealed to the district courts (Nordhaus 1932). This number is so low because there were very few license revocations in the nascent years of the Commission.

7. 281 U.S. 464 (1930). The opinion was actually a dismissal of a writ of certiorari previously granted.

Devanter's analysis. Some sixty years later Ronald Cass (1989, 83) was more direct, referring to the justice's reasoning as a "brief, cryptic opinion" and contending, "The *General Electric* decision moves from predicates that are not clearly established to inarticulate legal precepts to problematic conclusions."

Whether or not it was a sound decision, as a result of the *General Electric* ruling and the other problems associated with the original provisions of Section 16, Congress amended the 1927 act on July 1, 1930.[8] The revised law limited review of agency orders to questions of law. Agency findings of fact, review of which generated the controversy in the *General Electric* case, were to be final.[9] The main effect of this ruling was that when the agency exercised administrative discretion, its actions were not reviewable by the courts. Additionally, the 1930 amendment directly addresses the Supreme Court's reluctance to review lower court rulings by denoting that the Supreme Court has the right to such review.

While Congress hoped that these provisions would alleviate the problems that had arisen, contemporary analysts were not so certain. For example, Schmeckebier contended at the time,

> It remains to be seen whether this is sufficient. The mere conferring of reviewing authority does not necessarily change the character of the proceedings; if they were administrative before, they are not judicial now. (1932, 59)

Apparently, however, these new provisions satisfied the Supreme Court, for in 1933 the Court ruled in *FRC v. Nelson Brothers Bond and Mortgage Company* that the earlier defects had been rectified.[10]

As Cass (1989) portrays it, the revised law addressed each of the three main problems that resulted from the original law. First, it gave the right of appeal to anyone affected by a grant *or* denial of a radio license, thereby eliminating the problem in the 1927 act of what exactly constituted a denial. Second, it expanded standing, giving the right to appeal to all those parties whose interests were affected by the decision on another party's application. And finally, as just discussed, it addressed the dilemma raised by the Supreme Court by (1) vesting initial review exclusively in the Court

---

8. *U.S. Statutes at Large* 46 (1930): 844. The amendment, H.R. 12599, was introduced on May 24, 1930, and passed both houses of Congress one month later. Evidence of congressional or interest group preferences on this issue is extremely limited; there are no hearings or debates, and the committee reports are each less than two pages long.

9. Unless, of course, the commission was found to have acted in an "arbitrary and capricious" manner. For a discussion of such a case, see Edelman 1950, 63.

10. 9 U.S. 266 (1933).

of Appeals of the District of Columbia, thereby obviating the constitutional question of whether the local district court could review the agency's orders, (2) restricting the appellate court to decide questions of law only, and (3) specifically allowing Supreme Court review.

This revised law, then, provided the baseline that existed when political actors began moving toward legislation on what would become the Communications Act of 1934. What originally had been a limited yet extensive set of review powers—limited in the sense that only a specifically delineated set of decisions was reviewable and few participants had standing, extensive in the sense that the courts had considerable leeway to determine not only whether the agency had acted properly but also whether the agency had reached a "correct" decision—had been revised to loosen the limitations while corralling the extent to which courts could act.

Issues in the 1934 Act

Given this past history, it is apparent that the exact specification of judicial review was a matter of some dispute. It is therefore no surprise that this controversy continued during the debates over the Communications Act of 1934 and the bills leading up to this act. In fact, as mentioned earlier, judicial review was one of the issues over which there was the most disagreement.[11]

A measure of the concern over judicial review can be found in the hearings on S. 2910, held before the Senate Committee on Interstate Commerce in March 1934.[12] The chair of the Federal Radio Commission, E. O. Sykes, devoted a good portion of his testimony to suggestions for revising the newly proposed appeals section, which provided for appeal of certain decisions to district courts.[13] Sykes argued that those whose license application renewals were refused and those whose applications were revoked should have the right to appeal commission decisions to the Court of Appeals of the District of Columbia. Sykes gave two reasons for this suggestion, which effectively would have caused the new act to look

---

11. This disagreement is partly because legislators, to minimize opposition and ensure passage of the bill, left most controversial questions to be addressed by the agency in a report to be issued at a later time to Congress. As Senator Clarence Dill observed at the time, "If we leave out the controversial matters the bill can be passed at this session; otherwise it cannot" (quoted in Rosen 1980, 176). See also House Committee on Interstate and Foreign Commerce, *Regulation of Interstate and Foreign Communications by Wire and Radio, or for Other Purposes.* 73d Cong., 2d sess., 1 June 1934, 1850, 3; and G. Robinson 1989a, 3.

12. Detailed accounts of differences between legislative proposals can be found in chapter 6.

13. This portion of testimony is very difficult to figure out, due to Sykes's elliptical use of the English language. As best I can tell, it would have subjected all appeals—radio and telephone alike—to ICC-style provisions (i.e., those currently applicable to telephone).

like the 1927 act as amended. First, he argued, "A single court has become well informed concerning a technical subject."[14] A more important reason, however, was that the omission of such a provision would have hurt *existing* stations: "Where the Commission enters an order affecting the renewal of a radio-station license or the revocation thereof *the right to existence of a radio station is involved.*"[15] Sykes's argument was that neglecting to include such a provision would redound to the detriment of existing stations.

This example dovetails nicely with the argument, made by several observers and discussed in the previous chapter, that the commission at this time attempted to secure its position by favoring established interests at every turn. And in a way, these interests repaid the favor by becoming more supportive of the commission form of regulation in the 1930s:[16]

> The principal business witness who enthusiastically endorsed the unification of communications regulation and the prompt creation of the FCC was David Sarnoff of RCA. As the most powerful radio network, it had much to gain from the establishment of a permanent commission that would license all new applicants for radio stations. *From RCA's perspective anything that increased entry barriers into radio was to the good.* (Stone 1991, 279; emphasis added)[17]

And as we have seen, the general impression of most observers is that the Federal Radio Commission did not disappoint the interests that supported it.[18]

During the same hearings, the argument that the appeal provisions of S. 2910 had to be changed was made even more forcefully by Henry A. Bellows, chair of the NAB's Legislative Committee. Bellows, noting that S. 2910 relied on provisions like those previously applicable to common carriers, stressed that

---

14. Senate Committee on Interstate Commerce, *Hearings before the Committee on Interstate Commerce, United States Senate, on S. 2910,* 73d Cong., 2d sess., 9 March 1934, 44.

15. Ibid.; emphasis added.

16. By 1932 the commission format seemed favorable and the industry had stabilized to the point where it decided to seek permanent legislation to protect the status quo (McChesney 1994).

17. It should be acknowledged that while broadcasters favored creation of the FCC, AT&T very much opposed the creation of the agency. As Stone argues, "The law establishing the FCC was intended to be relatively uncontroversial. But on the other hand, it was expected to be a prelude to more drastic regulation that would follow an FCC investigation of telephone practices. . . . AT&T's opposition to the enactment of what became the Communications Act of 1934 stemmed, in part, from the fear that worse would follow" (1991, 276).

18. It is especially significant that RCA—which was still in the business of manufacturing and selling receivers—clearly preferred increased barriers to entry.

the most far-reaching and, we believe, potentially disastrous change proposed in this bill [is] the denial under certain circumstances of any right of appeal to the courts.[19]

Bellows further asserted that the radio industry needed provisions for review that were completely separate from those that would cover the common carriers, and that failure to include such separate provisions would cause serious harm to the existing radio industry:[20]

> [Y]ou have apparently created a situation in which many of the cases, many of the most important cases, which come before the Radio Commission and which would come before the new commission, could never be taken to the courts at all, and I do not believe that is desirable; I do not believe that it is necessary from any standpoint to do that. It is unquestionable that many of the cases which come before the Radio Commission and would come before the new commission are entirely different from the bulk of the cases which come before the Interstate Commerce Commission. They represent different types of service; they are applications for increases or extension of service; they are applications for new stations, and apparently those could none of them have been appealed, and we do not believe that that is intended or desirable.[21]

The solution, according to Bellows, was simple—Congress needed only to graft the provisions of Section 16, as amended, on to the proposed new act.[22]

While the controversy over the inclusion of separate provisions was an important issue in the early debates on the 1934 act, two other issues later occupied broadcasters' attention and dominated the debate over judicial review. First, there was the question of whether review should be

---

19. *Hearings on S. 2910,* 55.

20. The basis for Bellows's—and broadcasters'—concern was an earlier Supreme Court ruling (*Procter and Gamble Co. v. United States,* 225 U.S. 282 [1912]), which held that once the ICC denied an application, the decision was not appealable. See the statement of FRC general counsel D. M. Patrick, *Hearings on S. 2910,* 68. The impact of this decision is discussed in McFarland 1933, 122–23.

21. *Hearings on S. 2910,* 64.

22. Bellows's approach was a response to a clause in the proposed bill that called for the repeal of the 1927 act. He argued that since this repeal did not follow from the president's call for unified regulation of communications, it should be omitted and the new law should include the provisions found in the 1927 act. Then, he allowed, once the new commission had been able to study the situation, it might make the necessary changes to bring review of the two industries in line with each other.

vested only in the District of Columbia's Court of Appeals. The seemingly logical argument here was that local courts would favor local stations and not the commission (Cass 1989, 87).[23] Furthermore, the costs of traveling to Washington, both in terms of time and money, were not inconsequential at the time, providing another reason that radio stations would prefer to be able to appeal to a nearby court. And, in fact, most cases that were appealed but then dismissed by the courts were dismissed because of "failure to pay or deposit costs, or to file brief" (Nordhaus 1932, 459).

Interestingly, broadcasters took a position at odds with this apparently simple and obvious logic. In hearings on H.R. 8301, Bellows, again representing the NAB, proposed that the House amend its bill with regard to appeals so that *all* appeals would be taken to the Court of Appeals of the District of Columbia. The following colloquy, which demonstrates the NAB's position, is worth quoting at length:

Mr. Cole (D-MD): That means that all suits to review the orders of the Commission, pertaining to radio, would be exclusively in the District of Columbia?

Mr. Bellows: Exactly.

Mr. Cole: Not so as to all other subjects before the Commission.

Mr. Bellows: Not so as to the others.

Mr. Cole: Why lodge all of the litigation in the District of Columbia?

Mr. Bellows: Simply because in the entire development of the law as regards or affects radio communications, the District of Columbia courts have been the sole courts to which appeals might be taken, and through the Court of Appeals in the District of Columbia and [*sic*] apparently very sound body of law has been built up. . . . The present system appears to be working exceedingly well, and it is the feeling of most of the people who have considered it—I think it is the feeling of the Radio Commission itself—that a much more orderly development in Radio Commission cases, which is highly specialized, is provided by having those appeals centralized in one court.

Mr. Cole: I can see how the Radio Commission might well want all reviews of its orders right here in its home town. Under the bill before us the radio companies that have several stations on the Pacific coast, or in other parts of the country, wanting their day in court to have reviewed what this Commission might do would have to come all the way here to Washington.

---

23. See citations in chapter 3 regarding interest-group awareness of differences between courts.

Mr. Bellows: Exactly.

Mr. Cole: I think that is a pretty good monopoly for the lawyers of Washington, but too much of an imposition on the people in the rest of this country.

Mr. Bellows: I may say there has been a good deal of discussion from exactly the point of view that you bring up. In general the broadcasters have felt that since all hearings, or practically all hearings, are held here in Washington they would rather go ahead under the present law, that is, section 16 of the radio act, with the appeals brought here in Washington, than they would to have the jurisdiction for appeals distributed over the district courts.[24]

Thus, the main representative of radio broadcasters, the NAB, actually pushed Congress to concentrate review in one central location. While radio stations located far from Washington, D.C. would have faced hardships were review to be possible only in the District of Columbia Court of Appeals, commercial broadcasters obviously saw benefits in vesting review in a single court.[25]

The second issue concerned the scope of review. Recall that the 1930 amendment to the Radio Act resulted in a limiting of the scope of review; after passage of this amendment, courts were allowed to examine questions of law but not questions of fact. Such had *not* been the case in Section 16 of the 1927 act, of course, which leads one to question why some groups and members of Congress preferred a broader scope of review, both in the 1927 act and, now that a new agency was being created, in the new agency. The logic for radio interests would seem to be this: if fears still existed about actions that the agency might take, allowing the courts to examine the record de novo would present an additional opportunity for the station owners to achieve a favorable outcome.

Table 5.1 lists the central issues concerning review. What was the end result of the arguments over these issues? On the matter of which courts could be allowed to review appeals, the NAB lost—a clause was included to allow district courts to review certain actions. This outcome, however, seems favorable to noncommercial broadcasters. Educational and reli-

---

24. House Committee on Interstate and Foreign Commerce, *Hearings on H.R. 8301*, 73d Cong., 2d sess., 10 April 1934, 107–8.

25. An examination of NAB records reveals that there was some measure of eastern bias in its membership. All members of the NAB were obviously from radio stations. The officers were from the following cities: New York, Detroit, Boston (two), and Washington, D.C. In addition, 80 percent of the directors of the NAB (twelve out of fifteen) were from east of the Mississippi, and seven were from the East Coast. However, the membership was distributed more evenly among the five radio zones created by the 1929 Davis Amendment (roughly, Northeast, Mid-Atlantic, South, Midwest, and West).

TABLE 5.1.   Interest Groups and the Communications Act

Judicial Review Provisions	NAB Preferences
Scope of review	Broad (allow de novo review)
Reviewability	Any grants or denials
Court	Appeals Court of the District of Columbia
Standing	Anyone affected by an agency action
Time frame for appealing	Unknown

gious stations, much more likely to obtain—and afford—a favorable review in local district courts, likely were pleased by this outcome. However, given the FRC's track record with such stations, these groups also would have preferred, but did not get, a broad scope of review. And more importantly, the NAB was able to avoid the implementation of ICC-style review, which would have severely curtailed their ability to obtain review.

While the Communications Act did allow review of certain actions by district courts, Congress eventually decided to retain much of the style of review set forth in the 1930 amendments. As seen in table 5.2, courts explicitly had the right to review appeals of refusals and revocations, but review was limited to issues of law and not fact. Let us now examine the preferences of the interest groups in terms of the theoretical approaches laid out earlier.

Explaining the 1934 Act

One strong impression that emerges from the preceding case is that much of the battle over regulation of radio in the 1920s and 1930s can be seen in terms of interest-group struggle. An obvious split, and one on which many analysts have focused, is between commercial stations and noncommercial stations such as those operated by educational and religious institutions (e.g., Severin 1978). However, a careful reading of the case shows that, at least in the eyes of the existing stations, also important was the division between existing stations and potential entrants.

Of the five main types of judicial review provisions discussed earlier, the one on which we have the most direct evidence of preferences concerns the choice of the court to which appeals could be taken. As noted, at first glance one logical approach might assume that all stations would prefer to have review vested in the local district courts, which were more likely to be sympathetic to a local station.

All else equal, that is probably true. However, all else was not equal, and the representatives of the NAB strongly promoted vesting review in only the District of Columbia Court of Appeals. Two related explanations

TABLE 5.2. A Comparison of the Acts of 1927 and 1934

Judicial Review Provisions	1927 Act	1934 Act
Scope of review	Broad (de novo review)	Narrow (questions of law)
Reviewability	Revocations and refusals of licenses	Any grants or denials
Court	Appeals Court of the District of Columbia	Appeals Court of the District of Columbia or district courts
Standing	Only applicants whose licenses were refused or revoked	Anyone affected by an FCC action
Time frame for appealing	20 days	20 days

can be proposed for this position. First, some credence must be given to the NAB claim that this one court had developed a large amount of expertise in the area of radio law. In addition to the normative contention that a court with expertise in an area is likely to do a better job than is a novice court, expertise also reduces the uncertainty, and hence the cost, of seeking review. This feature of expertise is consistent with the argument presented in chapter 3 that members of the enacting coalition value certainty and consistent results.

Second, we also need to consider who would be more likely to be able to bear the costs associated with traveling to Washington to appeal an agency decision. While the costs would be high for existing stations, there is little doubt that the relative costs would be much higher for potential entrants—at times high enough to discourage any appeal at all.[26] Accordingly, the NAB's support for vesting review in a single court is not nearly so peculiar as it seems on first glance, but rather is consistent with the theoretical expectations spelled out in earlier chapters.

What of the other types of provisions? There is less direct evidence on some of these, but we still can attempt to explain the preferences of the groups. To do so, we turn now to the effects of experience, the legal regime, and theories of institutions. Again, let us start with the experiential approach.

As noted several times, most scholars who have studied radio regulation in the 1920s and 1930s have argued that first the FRC and later the FCC were dominated by the commercial broadcasters. Given this record

26. Recall the evidence in the previous chapter showing that powerful commercial stations would use judicial and administrative hearings, with their attendant high costs, to overwhelm smaller stations.

of favoritism, we might expect that the radio industry would prefer to give the agency wide latitude in making decisions.

What about the role of the courts in reviewing agency decisions? Nordhaus (1932) documents that while the judiciary was indeed a forum in which aggrieved parties could seek and find redress for what they considered unjust decisions, the courts did not overturn a preponderance of agency decisions. Action was taken in ninety-four cases between 1927 and 1932, and in only thirteen of these did the appellate court reverse the agency.[27] However, a secondary aspect of the appeals process is quite important here. While the Court of Appeals *directly* overturned the agency in only thirteen cases, in some seventeen other cases the action was dismissed by the appellant because the FRC changed its decision. And the court affirmed the judgment of the agency in only nineteen cases.[28] Thus, consistent with the previous chapter's argument that judicial review can affect an agency's choice of policy, court action proved to be an effective, if not foolproof, way to get a more favorable decision on an application.

Easily triggered judicial review, however, could be interpreted as a mixed blessing for the broadcast industry. On the one hand, recall that one of the main tenets of the commercial broadcasters' agenda was keeping new stations off the air (thereby minimizing interference). Allowing the courts to review refusals of applications by the FCC could be interpreted as going against the interests of the NAB, since it might add to interference and potentially reduce the NAB members' share of the market.

On the other hand, however, allowing the courts to review agency denials definitely was helpful in cases where a license renewal was refused, or where the commission modified the terms of a license in an unfavorable manner. Notably, almost all of the cases in which the court overturned the agency decisions involved *existing* stations, rather than applications for new stations. Indeed, only *one* of the thirty-one overturns involved an application for a new station! Allowing the courts to review all refusals (as opposed to none), was, on the whole, in the interest of the commercial broadcasters. Furthermore, it provides additional evidence on why the NAB preferred to keep decision-making power vested in the District of

---

27. There were a total of 118 appeals filed during this time period. Interestingly, only 3 were filed with the district courts; the rest were filed with the Court of Appeals for the District of Columbia. Of the 115 filed in the D.C. court, 21 were still pending at the time he wrote his article.

28. The breakdown of the 115 cases is as follows: 40 cases were dismissed by the appellants (of these, 18 were because the FRC changed its decision); 18 were dismissed by the court (usually for failure to pay fees); 13 agency decisions were reversed by the court; 19 were affirmed; 21 were pending; and 4 were interlocutory cases.

Columbia Court of Appeals. And it helps explain why Bellows feared a bill such as S. 2910, which would have sharply limited the types of agency decisions that could have been reviewed.

What does the legal regime tell us? An increasingly important trend at the time was to give agencies broad discretion and courts limited review (Nordhaus 1932, 472; Smulyan 1994,149). This trend is evidenced by referral to another agency, the Federal Trade Commission (FTC), which, typical of most such regulatory bodies, had not been seriously handicapped by court intervention (Davies 1923).[29] In addition, after the amendment of July 1, 1930 (passed in response to the *General Electric* case), the review of FRC decision making was similar to that of other regulatory agencies (Cushman 1941).

As far as guidelines for review were concerned, there is no record of interest-group preferences for review of law as opposed to review of fact. Perhaps this silence is explained by the unanimously applied standard of review based on law only, as noted by Cushman. For example, the standard had been contested several years earlier in the battle to create the FTC and was now the accepted norm for dealing with review of FTC decisions.

More likely, however, the lack of interest-group activity on this issue was based on the knowledge that the court had once previously struck down a clause allowing for review of facts.[30] If such review was permitted, the courts once again might have been limited in their ability to act as "judicial" entities.[31] Interest groups had little incentive to lobby for a clause that moved against the legal currents of the time and was likely to be struck down anyway.

Finally, what does the institutional approach tell us? In general, it is apparent that the commercial broadcast interests, given the emerging realist view of the courts and a constrained-actor view of bureaucracy,[32] would have opposed the implementation of ICC-style judicial review, which would have allowed for limited review, based on law, by the district courts. The existing commercial broadcasters had had favorable experiences with both the FRC and the District of Columbia Court of Appeals. The commission, as a constrained actor, was likely to make decisions in line with what the broadcasters preferred.

---

29. For a contrary view, see the work of E. Herring, who argues, "The story of the Federal Trade Commission shows how regulation can be weakened by unfavorable treatment at the hands of the courts" (1936,158).

30. Again, see the *General Electric* case.

31. In the *General Electric* decision, the Supreme Court ruled that an examination of questions of fact made the reviewing court no more than a higher administrative body.

32. These were the dominant views during this era and the perceptions that broadcasters would have formed through their experiences.

The commission, however, still had tremendously wide discretion under the public-interest standard of the legislation. In the event that the agency's decisions were *not* in the interests of broadcasters, they could be appealed to a court that had reversed nearly 40 percent of the cases that it decided. Based on these perspectives of the judiciary and bureaucracy, commercial broadcasters could be expected to—and did—favor a broader review by the D.C. court.

The Role of Uncertainty

Two points, drawing on the insights of chapter 3, will be made in this final section. First, the review provisions of the 1927 act can be construed as being somewhat more favorable to entrants than were the provisions of the 1934 act. Second, another reason for the changes in provisions over this time is the decreased uncertainty over the actions of the commission. As these points are related, they will be considered together.

In what way were the original review provisions more favorable to potential entrants? First of all, while standing was limited, it was *not* limited in a way that would harm stations attempting to get licenses. The later changes in this provision, it will be recalled, were to allow *existing* stations to appeal if an action on another license aggrieved or adversely affected them. The main desire of potential entrants was a chance to appeal if their license applications were refused, and the original provisions allowed for that.

Second, Section 16 did allow for only limited reviewability of agency decisions. Again, however, the needs of potential entrants in this regard were satisfied. The types of decisions of most concern to these stations were refusals of license applications, and such actions specifically were deemed reviewable by the Radio Act.

Third, the 1927 provisions specified a broad scope of review—that is, agency actions could be reviewed on either procedural *or* factual grounds. To repeat a point made earlier, potential entrants were extremely leery of the large amount of power held by the agency (Cushman 1941). At the same time, businesses felt a much higher degree of certainty about the probable actions of the courts.

All stations were worried about getting licenses when the FRC was created, and there was great uncertainty about what types of actions this powerful new agency would take.[33] Consequently, the review provisions reflected the fear of station owners that the agency would not act favorably

---

33. Even stations that already had been operating were worried about getting licenses, because the Radio Act specified that all existing station licenses were to expire sixty days after its approval (Schmeckebier 1932, 23).

toward them. If the commission were to act in such a manner, these station owners wanted recourse to the courts.

As stressed in chapter 2, the courts at this time were viewed as protectors of property rights. The legal regime was one in which the courts, seen as a staunch friend of business, opposed the unreasonable intrusion of the government into the affairs of business. When into this climate was thrown a new, powerful agency, it was only natural that it should be put under close review by the courts. On both the expected outcomes and the amount of uncertainty surrounding these outcomes, the courts were seen by radio station owners as preferable to the agency. On the matters of most interest to entrants, therefore, court protection from agency actions was afforded.

The review provisions in the 1934 act represent a quite different set of considerations. As I argued in the previous chapter, the power of commercial broadcasters had grown between 1927 and 1934. Not surprisingly, then, the preferences of these station owners, and to a large degree the provisions of the 1934 act, were a reflection of their goal to keep their own licenses while making it more difficult for others to enter the radio market.

To begin with, even though the legal regime was no longer one in which the judiciary was perceived as a strict Lochner-era protector of property rights, it was still an era in which courts were generally predisposed to protect businesses from unwarranted government interference. In other words, there was still a fair degree of certainty surrounding the potential actions of the courts. Thus, as exemplified by Bellows's testimony, the NAB viewed it as essential to the owners of existing stations that license revocations and "applications for increases or extensions of service" be reviewable.[34]

It can be seen from this testimony and others that members of the NAB wanted to make sure that owners of existing stations would have standing in other cases that might affect them. As seen earlier, the biggest fear of the members of the NAB was that they would be denied the ability to seek redress of perceived wrongs in the courts; thus, with respect to standing, they pushed for the inclusion of the provisions of Section 16 as amended.

The NAB also strongly urged Congress to vest initial review authority in the Court of Appeals of the District of Columbia. As explained earlier, several factors combine to explain this preference. First and foremost, the broadcasters sought to vest sole authority in the D.C. court because doing so would drastically reduce the amount of uncertainty about court decisions. Whereas the local district courts represented a set of unknowns,

34. The broadcaster's greater faith in the courts held true even given the much more favorable impression station owners now had of the commission. See *NAB Reports,* March 28, 1931.

the predisposition of the D.C. court—while often supportive of the agency—was known with a great degree of certainty. Second, the NAB also calculated that vesting review in this court alone would place a hardship on their opponents, as the financial situation of these opponents was, on average, not strong.

The 1934 act thus reflects political calculations while also reflecting changed political circumstances. Existing stations now were more worried about holding on to what they had gained, and this concern is reflected in their preferences over review provisions. In addition, the legal regime had changed—uncertainty over the actions of the commission was much reduced, after several years of substantive experience.[35] But it was still the case that while broadcasters now preferred more power in the hands of the agency, they still wanted at least a modicum of review. Then, in the event that the agency did not act according to their wishes, they might be able to get a more favorable decision from the court—and, more important, from a specific and friendly court, the District of Columbia Court of Appeals.

Conclusion

The political nature of judicial review provisions is apparent. These provisions were central to the politics of radio regulation in general and to the creation of the Federal Communications Commission in particular. Similarly clear is that interest groups pay a great deal of attention to these sorts of "details," as these groups know how important such details may be in the future. Furthermore, evidence demonstrates that groups act strategically when supporting such provisions. A group does not simply look at a provision in isolation, but rather also considers what effects a provision will have on its opponents. Finally, we saw that groups rely on experience, trends in the legal regime, and institutional models in determining which provisions are optimal and in resolving uncertainty about the potential actions of courts and the commission.

What is obviously missing so far is the role played by elected officials. Just as interest-group preferences were not determinative in the political battle over the structure of the FRC, nor were they determinative in the creation of judicial review provisions. In the next chapter I will turn to the role played by these elected officials.

---

35. The industry's attitude toward the agency had clearly improved as a result of the types of actions described in the previous chapter. As McChesney tartly suggests, "The industry was also quite content with the manner in which the FRC was stabilizing the airwaves for profitable exploitation" (1994, 128).

CHAPTER 6

Congress and the Provision of
Judicial Review

Interest groups are not alone in their attempts to structure judicial review provisions to achieve political advantage. Members of Congress also have the incentive to do so, based on their knowledge that the choices they make today will have a great effect on court-produced policy outcomes in the future.[1] In this chapter I will review Congress's role in communications policy in the early years of regulation. After this review I will detail the legislative development of the Communications Act of 1934, with a specific focus on the choices Congress made in structuring the provisions for review of agency decisions about radio.

In tracing through this history, several facets of Congress's interest in institutional design become apparent. Generally, whenever Congress was concerned with changing communications law, it considered carefully where decision-making authority should be placed. More specifically, in the case of the Communications Act, it focused a great deal of attention on the structure of judicial review.

This account ties into the theoretical framework of earlier chapters in several ways. To begin with, this chapter once again demonstrates that political considerations underlie decisions about the design of judicial review. Congress clearly paid attention to the different types of provisions that could be used and frequently debated these provisions. If Congress had not been interested in debating these provisions, the concerns of the NAB would have compelled them to do so. In fact, we shall see that the NAB was very vocal about these provisions, forcing Congress to take into account the interest-group context.[2] While Congress did not give the NAB

---

1. The president obviously has such an incentive, too. However, I should note that at least in the case of communications policy, President Roosevelt, despite calling for the unification of regulation, was most notable for his *lack* of involvement. Preoccupied with the more pressing issues of the Depression, he elected not to become involved in any of the fights surrounding radio (McChesney 1994, 181).

2. Because most members knew so little about communications policy, Congress was extremely dependent on the NAB for information about the effects of different features of the Communications Act. In addition, members of Congress wanted to *use* radio and thus were loathe to offend radio's most powerful companies.

everything it wanted, it did acquiesce on some of the most important issues.

Perhaps most important, this chapter demonstrates that Congress drew on various sources of information, discussed in earlier chapters, to discern the extent to which the actions of the new agency should be subjected to judicial review. In particular, much of the debate reflected institutional considerations. Congressional debate reflected a lingering concern over the legitimacy of independent agencies, as well as some uncertainty over the actions of these agencies. Congress certainly had had some experience with independent agencies by this point but very little experience in a policy area that was as technologically sophisticated or that changed as quickly as communications. So while experience had demonstrated that a commission could yield outcomes very favorable to Congress, many members still preferred proposals that would imbue the courts with broad review powers. Thus, an important issue was how to structure review so that it would provide outcomes closest to what Congress preferred.

Congress and Communications Policy in the 1920s

An early overview of Congress's role in the regulation of radio reached the following conclusion:

> Ever since the first regularly scheduled public radio-broadcast in 1920, Congress has played a unique and central role in the control of radio-broadcasting. As an agency for legislation, it has created the regulatory mechanisms under which the radio industry functions, and it has written the laws which govern this important area of communications. Congress, in fact, has set the pattern within which the various groups and interests operate, subject, of course, to the working rules of the capitalist order. In doing so, Congressmen have been at the beck and call of millions of constituents interested in radio as listeners or broadcasters, as educators or clergymen, as big or little business men. (Friedrich and Sternberg 1943, 797)

In this quote, the authors highlight the high level of congressional interest in communications—and the high level of interest in Congress's interest. However, the standard "textbook" portrayal of Congress's role in the regulation of communications presents a quite different view. In fact, Congress often is portrayed as both reactive to and unable to deal with the technical complexity of radio regulation in the first three decades of this century. Even the authors just quoted agree with this view, to an extent:

But even a cursory study of Congressional debates or hearings reveals the inadequacies of Congress in handling matters of technical complexity. Actually, Congress has always been a step behind technical progress in the radio field, following new developments with legislation only when these have grown big and important enough to demand the attention of Congress. These difficulties may be inherent in the nature of radio and in the nature of our Congressional system as well. (Friedrich and Sternberg 1943, 798)[3]

What might the textbook view of congressional inaction look like? After passing laws in 1910 and 1912, laws that provided for the registration of radio transmission, Congress did not pass another major law until 1927, when it created the Federal Radio Commission (FRC) as a temporary agency.[4] This long gap was not due to a lack of clamor for legislation—indeed, there were repeated calls for legislation all throughout the 1920s. It was instead due to the inability of Congress to legislate in a rapidly changing medium characterized by a high level of technical complexity. Legislation was ultimately passed only when Congress's hand was forced by a pair of court decisions that threw the radio industry into chaos and threatened its long-term stability.[5]

Next, according to this view, Congress shirked its responsibility to seriously review and reconsider the supposedly temporary FRC. Instead,

---

3. This account is far from alone in stressing the difficulties imposed by the technical complexity of radio. For another account, see, for example, Fainsod and Gordon 1941, 380. A telling example of representatives' lack of understanding of radio is revealed by one member's worry that if radio equipment were to be installed in Congress, some anarchists "would send something through it and blow us all out of here" (quoted in Smulyan 1994, 142).

4. As discussed earlier, the FRC was originally created for a period of only one year, during which time it was to hold the bulk of regulatory authority (although the secretary of commerce still retained some purely administrative powers, such as receiving applications for station licenses). After one year, all authority was to revert back to the Department of Commerce.

Unfortunately, while several authors have suggested reasons for this division of responsibility, no accounts are completely satisfactory and none are rigorous. Most accounts simply refer to the necessity of a compromise in order to ensure that legislation was passed before the end of the legislative session. Given that this legislation set the path for all future actions, this is a surprising gap in the literature on the history of broadcast regulation in the 1920s. While this is an extremely worthwhile future project, I shall not pursue it here.

5. The two main decisions were *Hoover v. Intercity Radio, Inc.,* 286 F. 1003 (1923) and *United States v. Zenith Radio Corporation,* 12 F.2d 616 (1926). In addition, as J. Herring and Gross (1936, 241) discovered, an earlier situation, in which the attorney general concluded that existing laws conferred no discretionary power upon the secretary of commerce, had portended the results of these later cases.

each year it routinely reapproved the agency for another year.[6] Then, although it had the opportunity to rewrite and improve regulation of radio when President Roosevelt called for the creation of a new agency to regulate all communications activities, Congress's feeble response was to mindlessly transfer the existing regulations for radio into the 1934 act. So even though regulation of radio was the main focus of the 1934 act, Congress, with a minimum of discussion and even less effort, actually merely ratified the status quo in this legislation.[7]

There are clearly some truths to this stylized account. For example, after 1912 Congress did not pass a major radio bill until 1927, despite repeated calls throughout the 1920s for legislation. However, several historians have convincingly rejected the simplistic view that Congress was uninterested in radio regulation or was unable to deal with it because of the technical complexity of the medium.[8] There were always at least two obstacles to the passage of legislation. First of all, there was considerable disagreement about whether there was such an urgent need for regulation. While on the surface it seemed like all radio interests agreed on the need for legislation, in actuality there were always enough dissenters to this view—powerful dissenters—that it is by no means surprising that attempts to pass legislation were not successful.[9]

Second, even among those who saw the need for legislation, the structure of regulation—that is, the location of regulatory authority—was very controversial. The failure to pass legislation, therefore, was not due to lack of effort or interest on the behalf of Congress. During the 1920s, more than a dozen bills addressing the 1912 law were introduced and debated.[10]

---

6. I discuss this in greater detail in the next section.

7. See, for example, G. Robinson 1989a, who refers to "the extensive—one could say 'wholesale'—borrowing from earlier statutes with little or no new explanation or gloss of meaning" (5). Also see Temin 1987, 11, 29. For a different point of view, one consistent with the argument presented in this book, see McChesney: "The Communications Act of 1934, far from constituting an addendum to the Radio Act of 1927, was promulgated and passed on its own terms and in its own context" (1994, 253).

8. In contrast to the paucity of materials on the 1934 act—McChesney's wonderful 1994 account excepted—there are several good accounts of the politics of radio regulation in the 1920s. Probably the best of these is Rosen 1980. See also Smulyan 1994. Loeb (1978) provides an excellent overview of the bills dealing with telecommunications during this time.

9. Rosen (1980) argues that the perception of an agreement was only a mirage. In looking more closely at the different interests, he finds substantial disagreement among the major radio interests as to the necessity of regulation.

10. A House report reveals that between 1921 and 1927, twelve bills were introduced to replace the act of 1912 and another four were introduced to amend the act. Ten of these bills were introduced in the Senate; only in the House, however, were any bills reported out of committee. See House 1958, esp. n. 29. See T. Berry 1937 for a comprehensive list of all congressional attempts to pass communications legislation in the thirty years preceding the Com-

The failure to pass legislation during this time was not due to any lack of activity, effort, or concern by Congress, but rather was due mostly to the inability to agree on the serious political questions about the need for regulation and the location of regulatory authority.[11]

By 1927, when the need for regulation had become clear, the more serious and basic rift was over whether regulatory authority should be vested in a newly created independent agency or whether it should be vested in the Department of Commerce, which had been responsible for what regulation there was in the wake of the acts of 1910 and 1912. Members of the Senate, and most radio interests, preferred to leave authority with the Department of Commerce. On the other hand, members of the House, led by several Democrats, pushed for the creation of an independent commission, no doubt partly because they feared giving Herbert Hoover, who was secretary of commerce and a likely Republican presidential candidate, such power over radio.

The concern over the location of regulatory authority, however, transcended this specific policy area. One of the primary concerns of members of Congress in creating administrative bodies in the 1920s and into the 1930s was the *legitimacy* of the institutions they were creating.[12] The wide leverage given to courts by the 1927 act undoubtedly was due in part to this general suspicion of independent agencies. For those members who supported regulation by an independent regulatory commission, broad judicial review provisions may well have been the price they needed to pay to achieve their goal.

Congress, the Communications Act, and Judicial Review

The Communications Act of 1934 is well known for the public-interest rationale that forms the core of the law. While the legislation is quite clear in directing the Federal Communications Commission (FCC) to pursue the public interest—"The Commission, if public convenience, interest, or necessity will be served thereby . . . shall grant to any applicant therefor a station license provided for by this Act"[13]—it completely fails to specify what this public interest is or how it should be discovered. Consequently,

---

munications Act. Berry identifies twenty laws and resolutions in the 67th Congress (1921–23), thirteen laws and resolutions in the 68th Congress, and eighteen in the 69th Congress.

    11. The technical nature of radio was also an obvious impediment.

    12. Le Duc and McCain (1970) cite Roscoe Pound, FRC Commissioner Orestes Caldwell, and John Dickenson as prominent examples of legal scholars who contributed to the view of "administrative regulation as an evil growth upon the body politic" (393).

    13. Communications Act of 1934, 47 U.S.C., sec. 307(a).

the act is often described as being vague, mainly due to the centrality of the public-interest standard. And the vagueness of the legislation is, arguably, reflected by the ease of its passage—the final bill was brought to a voice vote, as there was virtual certainty it would pass.

However, just as the inability of Congress to pass a law before 1927 should not be taken as a sign of congressional inattentiveness, but rather as a function of broader political currents, the easy passage of the Communications Act of 1934 should not be taken as evidence of inattentiveness or blind support for the status quo. Nor should the vague nature of the general mandate be taken as a sign that there was no controversy.

While it is clear that the majority of the provisions of the act were not controversial, that is partly because members agreed to ignore these controversial issues in order to facilitate passage of the bill. Senator Clarence Dill observed at the time, "If we leave out the controversial matters, the bill can be passed at this session of Congress; otherwise it cannot" (House 1958, 28). This desire to avoid controversy was based in part on President Franklin D. Roosevelt's message to Congress in early 1934, which called for the transfer of FRC and ICC authority to a new agency, and which also suggested deferring any difficult questions to the new agency.[14] The House Committee on Interstate and Foreign Commerce even acknowledged this goal in one of its final reports:

> The bill is largely based upon existing legislation and except for the change of administrative authority does not very greatly change or add to existing law; most controversial questions are held in abeyance for a report by the new commission recommending legislation for their solution.[15]

This acknowledgement, like Senator Dill's comment, revealed a strong commitment to quick passage of the bill.

Perhaps the most controversial issue was the Wagner-Hatfield amendment, which was introduced on the floor of the Senate on May 15, 1934. This amendment, which would have required the allotment of 25 percent of all frequencies to nonprofit agencies such as religious or educational organizations, was defeated 42–23 after heated debate. Many members

---

14. On this point, see House 1958, 27–28. Roosevelt's message can be found in several places, including Senate, *Message from the President of the United States Recommending that Congress Create a New Agency to Be Known as the Federal Communications Commission,* 73d Cong., 2d sess., 20 February 1934, S. Doc. 144.

15. House Committee on Interstate and Foreign Commerce, "Regulation of Interstate and Foreign Communications by Wire and Radio, or for Other Purposes," 73d Cong., 2d sess., 1 June 1934, H. Rept. 1850, 3. This report was issued by Sam Rayburn's committee.

who voted against this amendment evidently preferred to keep this issue separate from the larger question of how to organize regulation. To this end, the Senate accepted Dill's proposal to put the issue on the table of the future commission, rather than attempting to write it into legislation and in the process killing the bill.[16]

Despite the desire to avoid controversy, certain issues that were ultimately included in the act were debated extensively within Congress. One such controversial issue was the exact nature of judicial review. While agreement was eventually reached, the provisions were repeatedly debated during discussions and hearings about communications policy.[17]

The brevity and lack of specificity of the actual bill therefore should not be construed as meaning that controversy did not exist. First, some of the controversial issues were simply avoided or consciously held in abeyance. Second, as the debates prior to the passage of legislation show, there were issues of controversy, and it is to one of these controversial issues—the nature of judicial review—that we will turn shortly.[18] First, however, let us look again at the path taken from the 1927 act to the 1934 act.

After the 1927 Act

To reiterate, most accounts of the Communications Act have emphasized either the vague nature of the bill or similarities between the act and existing regulations. And even many esteemed scholars who have studied the passage of this act in detail have tended to give short shrift to the matter of judicial review (e.g., E. Herring 1936; Cushman 1941). In this section I will first discuss some of the efforts to pass legislation in the years leading up to the passage of the 1934 act and then will detail the controversies surrounding the specification of judicial review.[19]

---

16. The next year the FCC recommended that no slots on the spectrum be set aside for educational stations. Their ruling was based on the grounds that the existing stations already were doing a satisfactory job of providing educational programming. See McChesney 1994 for an in-depth analysis of the Wagner-Hatfield amendment, the FCC's subsequent report, and the torrid behind-the-scenes battles between commercial broadcasters and the broadcast reform movement.

17. One could argue that the fact that agreement was reached implies that judicial review was not one of the more controversial issues. I disagree. Instead, I contend that controversial but *nonessential* issues were left out (i.e., the allocation of a certain percentage of stations for educational purposes); judicial review provisions were both controversial *and* essential.

18. Almost all of the dissatisfaction with the status quo was voiced by members lacking in power. Party leaders and relevant committee chairs overwhelmingly favored the status quo and prevented almost all reform legislation from reaching the floor (McChesney 1994).

19. On the era between the acts of 1927 and 1934, see House 1958, Cushman 1941, E. Herring 1936, Rosen 1980, McChesney 1994, Coase 1959, and Friedrich and Sternberg 1943.

As mentioned earlier, in the Radio Act of 1927 Congress specified that the Radio Commission would be in charge of licensing for one year, after which time this authority would revert to the Department of Commerce and the commission would become an appellate body. However, the first years of the commission were sufficiently unsettled that Congress felt unable to evaluate whether the agency should be abolished or whether the existing arrangement should be extended.[20] Because of this uncertainty, most members of Congress felt the commission should be given more time in which to show what it could do.[21] In reaction, Congress twice passed laws extending the existing setup, both times postponing a permanent decision.[22] Eventually, late in 1929, Congress apparently decided that if it was going to deliberate each year only to reach the conclusion that the status quo should be extended, it might as well sink the status quo into more permanent legislative concrete. Prodded by President Hoover, who now favored "the reorganization of the Radio Commission into a permanent body from its temporary status," Congress finally acted positively, introducing legislation giving licensing power to the commission indefinitely.[23] This measure was passed almost without opposition by each house and was quickly signed into law by Hoover.[24]

Before moving on, it is worthwhile to note some of the activities that took place during the renewals of the FRC. Although these debates did not directly revolve around the nature of judicial review, they provide a revealing account of the views of different actors toward regulation.

To begin with, radio interests initially did not seem particularly worried that the Federal Radio Commission might be abolished. Representatives of several radio industry giants stressed that the Department of Commerce might still be the better institution in which to lodge regulation. For

---

20. For an account of the bizarre circumstances in the first few years of the FRC, see, among others, Rosen 1980, 107; and Barnouw 1966, 211. Barnouw remarked, "In almost every respect the career of the Federal Radio Commission was weird, to the point of straining belief" (1966, 211). Among other things, the commission was plagued by inadequate funding, a high mortality rate and a low confirmation rate among commissioners, and a lack of staff and office space.

21. This is the standard view of why Congress chose to extend the existing arrangement. Rosen offers a slightly different view, arguing that in addition to the realization that the FRC needed more time to demonstrate its worth, another dimension was that "radio control still confused a good many of the lawmakers" (1980, 127).

22. The first of these, which was passed on March 28, 1928, and extended the 1927 act to March 16, 1929, was part of the Davis amendment (*U.S. Statutes at Large* 45 [1928]: 373). The second, which was passed on March 4, 1929, extended the act until December 31, 1929 (*U.S. Statutes at Large* 45 [1929]: 1559).

23. The quote is from the President's annual message to Congress (*Congressional Record,* 71st Cong., 2d sess., 1929, 72, pt. 1:25).

24. *U.S. Statutes at Large* 46 (1929): 50.

example, at hearings before Congress, a representative for the Radio Corporation of America (RCA) argued for a return of regulation to the secretary of commerce.[25] The Radio Manufacturers' Association also voiced little concern that the life of the commission might not be extended, especially if the alternative would be allowing control to pass back to the able hands of the Department of Commerce.[26] Similarly, the National Association of Broadcasters (NAB) stridently criticized the commission form of governmental control.

All of this activity reinforces the notion that while the industry in the 1920s wanted some regulation, it remained—at least initially—somewhat distrustful of the independent-commission format. The radio industry had lost the battle over structure in the White Act of 1927 (it had opposed the creation of an independent commission but was defeated by senators who favored such a creation), and it continued to oppose the commission form of regulation.[27] The leading scholar of regulatory agencies during the 1930s lends support to this notion:

> It was widely felt that the power to grant, revoke, or modify station licenses, a power to be exercised under the vague guiding standard of the public interest, convenience, and necessity, was too vitally important to be exercised by any administrative body without judicial review of the most complete scope. Accordingly, the Court of Appeals of the District of Columbia was authorized to review the decisions of the proposed radio commission in license matters and to reach its own independent judgment regarding the soundness and justice of the commission's action. (Cushman 1941, 308–9)

This argument is buttressed by the testimony of many members of Congress. New Jersey Representative Lehlbach, for example, strenuously objected to the commission form of government:

> . . . As a general principle, I am opposed to independent commissions in our Government and did not look with favor upon the creation of one for the regulation and control of radio. . . . The creation of independent commissions performing administrative functions and not subject to the guidance and control of the Chief Executive was an afterthought and not contemplated in the original structure of our

---

25. Senate Committee on Interstate Commerce, *Hearings on S. 4937,* 70th Cong., 2d sess., 1929, 143.

26. *New York Times,* 22 January 1929, 32; cited in E. Herring 1936, 161.

27. By 1934, however, the radio industry was strongly supportive of the unification of communications regulation and the creation of a new independent commission.

Government. In most instances it has not been productive of beneficent results.[28]

Lehlbach's comments, Cushman's observations, and several other sources all support the argument that a strong measure of judicial protection was necessary to get a compromise that allowed the creation of an independent commission.[29]

In reviewing the Radio Commission, then, the location of authority again was a matter of great importance. When the 1927 scheme came up for evaluation, there were at least four possible outcomes (Cushman 1941, 314–15). First, the arrangement created in 1927, which made the FRC a temporary agency, could have been made permanent.[30] Second, the Department of Commerce could have been made the primary regulator, with the commission turned into an appellate body.[31] Third, all powers could have been given to the Department of Commerce. And fourth, all powers could have been given to a permanent commission.

Initially, the first two possibilities seemed most likely to occur. But eventually, as we have seen, the fourth outcome obtained—all power was vested in a permanent commission. A plausible explanation is that "legislative inertia" was the primary cause—it was simply easiest to let the agency continue to do what it had been set up to do (Cushman 1941, 315). This explanation dovetails with the later assessment of the situation by one of the legislative participants, Clarence Dill. In his memoirs, Dill (1970) argues that senators really knew that once the commission was created, it would not easily be removed or disbanded, and thus that the whole view of the 1927 arrangement as a compromise is mistaken. But even this explanation ignores the fact that the *easiest* solution would have been to do *nothing,* in which case the second scenario listed in the previous paragraph would have obtained.

Shortly after the FRC was given permanent status, one other piece of

---

28. *Congressional Record,* 69th Cong., 2d sess., 1927, 68, pt. 3, 2570.

29. One of the ways in which Representative White tried to make legislation more appealing to broadcasters was by including a provision for appeal, a provision that previously had not been included (Rosen 1980, 73).

30. Cushman lists several arguments in favor of extending the original arrangement: the commission had not yet had enough time in which to be fairly judged; the licensing of stations was a quasi-judicial function and therefore should not be given to an agency; the industry would be severely disrupted by handing over power to the Department of Commerce, as this executive agency was not yet equipped to handle such tasks; and finally, it was likely that all orders and decisions of the Department of Commerce would be appealed to the Federal Radio Commission, so the commission—which would consist of experts—might as well be given authority to make the decisions in the first place.

31. This was the ostensible goal of the compromise that resulted in the 1927 act.

legislation significant to the purposes of this study was passed. This bill, which was discussed in much more detail in chapter 5, was passed with very little notice and was a reaction to problems discovered with the provisions for judicial review written into the 1927 act.[32] It provided for several changes in the appeals process. First, appeals now could be made only to the Court of Appeals of the District of Columbia. Second, all stations that were adversely affected by a licensing decision had the right to appeal. Third, the court was now prohibited from considering a case de novo and would instead have to rely on the commission's findings. And fourth, the new bill expressly provided for review by the Supreme Court.

Establishing the FCC

The idea to create a single agency to regulate all communications was first suggested in 1929 by a Republican senator, James Couzens of Mississippi. Couzens was the sponsor of a Senate bill, S. 6, that proposed to create such an agency. Writing at the time, he argued,

> There is legitimate contention against the creation of new boards, bureaus, and commissions in Washington. I have been one of those who have so contended, and I am still one of those who oppose the development of bureaucracy in government. However, criticism should depend upon the particular question at issue. In this case, I do not think there can be sound criticism of the commission form of control. I have favored the creation of a Commission on Communications. This does not involve the creation of a new commission, but rather merely calls for the substitution of one commission for another commission. (1930, 261)

While acknowledging the arguments that typically had been made against such commissions, Couzens made it clear that he preferred creating an independent regulatory agency to using an executive department:

> In any plan which would place the administration of radio in the Department of Commerce or any other department, there is the certainty of one-man rule. . . . In dealing with the radio, the government must dispose of franchises of tremendous value. . . . Because of this,

---

32. The law, Public Law 71–494, 71st Cong., 2d sess. (1 July 1930), originated as H.R. 12599. See the previous chapter for more detail on the nature of changes made by this bill and also for a description of the bill's "causes." Surprisingly, although the bill made some major changes, the committee reports provide no insights and there are no debates in the congressional record. The legislative history on this amendment is empty.

there should be determined opposition to turning this authority over to one individual. (1930, 261–62)

He concluded,

In the establishment of a Commission on Communications we have a proposal for a definite tenure of office and a permanent body. We have the hope that gradually this Commission will develop until it will gain the confidence and respect which is had by the Interstate Commerce Commission. (1930, 262–63)

Couzens's bill was not reported out of committee, reportedly because the other members of the committee thought the bill was premature (Cushman 1941). However, his bill placed the idea of unifying the regulation of communications on the public agenda to stay, and over the next few years the idea gradually gained more support.

The first serious, if ultimately unsuccessful, attempt to at least partially unify regulation of communications was made with the introduction of H.R. 7716. This bill, submitted in the 72nd Congress, proposed combining the Radio Division of the Department of Commerce with the FRC.

Although this bill did pass both houses of Congress, it fell victim to a pocket veto by President Hoover. Because Hoover used a pocket veto, there was no formal explanation of why he chose not to sign the bill. However, because the bill did not bring together all communications regulation—it left out areas covered by the ICC—one plausible explanation is that the bill did not go far enough in unifying regulation (Cass 1989). Despite being vetoed, the bill is still important because many of the provisions of this bill eventually ended up in the 1934 act.[33]

Most of these provisions of H.R. 7716 are outside of the scope of this study—for example, the stipulation in Section 5 dealing with the painting of radio towers. But one notable section of this bill was Section 10, which amended the judicial review provisions of the 1927 act.[34] In this section it was proposed that stations whose licenses were revoked (and also owners

---

33. On the similarity of H.R. 7716 to S. 3285 and the eventual 1934 act, see Senate Committee on Interstate Commerce, *Communications Act of 1934,* 73d Cong., 2d sess., 17 April 1934, S. Rept. 781, 6–10. H.R. 7716 is discussed in Senate Committee on Interstate Commerce, *Report on H.R. 7716,* 72d Cong., 2d sess., S. Rept. 1045; and House Committee on Interstate and Foreign Commerce, *Report on H.R. 7716,* 72d Cong., 2d sess., 1932, H. Rept. 221.

34. Another important debate over procedural "details" in this bill concerned whether stations or the FRC should have the burden of proof in the suspending of licenses. Bellows argued for the NAB that the FRC should have this burden.

who had been fined) be given the right to appeal to the local district court or circuit court of appeals. It also specified that judicial review should be based on questions of either law or fact, a broad guideline that reflected the continued concern of some members about policy-making by an independent agency.[35]

This arrangement for judicial review was similar to the original 1927 act in that all questions about radio law did not have to go to the District of Columbia Court of Appeals. The justification for this arrangement was given in the conference committee's report: "This is especially important from the standpoint of building up a series of legal interpretations of radio law by different inferior courts of the United States."[36]

The committee report went on to promote the proposed provisions as

> a simpler and more efficatious [*sic*] procedure in appeals. Your committee has added provisions giving the licensee whose license is revoked, or the owner who has been fined, the right to appeal in the lower district court instead of being required to come in to Washington, D.C., to prosecute his appeal in the district court of the District of Columbia. This is of particular advantage to the owners of small stations located a long distance from the District of Columbia.[37]

While many members of Congress favored this approach, others voiced concern about it. In particular, Louis Caldwell, speaking for the American Bar Association, argued that the provisions of the bill would run afoul of the same ground as did the original 1927 provisions, as the bill would allow review of law *and* fact and would therefore preclude Supreme Court review (*NAB Reports,* December 22, 1932).

On the matter of which courts could hear appeals, there was considerable disagreement. In particular, a clause allowing for appeal of revocations or fines to any of the circuit courts drew the attention of Senator White:

---

35. Representative McGugin offered a strong statement of this point of view: "I do not care how able the members of the commission may be. I do not care what commission it may be. I believe it is contrary to true liberty and true justice to leave the final decree in the hands of any bureau. I want final consideration vested in an appellate court consisting of the United States court in our own States" (*Congressional Record,* 72d Cong., 1st sess., 1932, 75, pt. 4:3693).

36. House Committee on Interstate and Foreign Commerce, Report on H.R. 7716, 72d Cong., 2nd sess., 1932, H. Rept. 221 (the original was in the conference report to accompany H.R. 7716, submitted by Rep. Davis of Tennessee). This quote also can be found in House 1958, 24. Recall from the previous chapter, however, that this was exactly what the NAB did *not* want.

37. Quoted in *NAB Reports,* January 21, 1933.

When the 1927 Act was written, it was more or less a pioneering task. There was no body of radio law in the United States, and those active in framing the legislation were going into new and unexplored fields. I have always believed that it was as important that there should be certainty with respect to the radio law. . . . I do not like at all the suggestion that we are going to have these decisions by the various Circuit Courts of Appeal of the United States. We have nine circuits. We may have nine different constructions of law all at the same time. . . . I think it is vastly more important that there should be a single tribunal determining the law with respect to radio, at least in the inception of the development of radio law.[38]

A response from Senator Dill indicated a contrary attitude:

I think it will be to the benefit of radio that the judges of the nine circuit courts of appeal may pass on these questions, rather than that one court of appeals in the District shall have a monopoly upon such decisions. There may have been justification for that when the original law was written, but radio has reached such proportions that there will have to be new interpretations. . . .[39]

As we will see, this issue of which courts should hear appeals was revisited in the following year.

Roosevelt and the Unification of Communications Regulation

Although H.R. 7716 never became law, its cardinal concept of a single communications commission soon received a great impetus when President Roosevelt began to support it. Roosevelt saw that control over communications was at the time divided among several different places—the Radio Commission, the Department of Commerce, the postmaster general, the ICC, and the president (through the Interdepartmental Radio Advisory Committee). Control, therefore, was neither unified nor centralized (Cushman 1941).

Roosevelt asked Secretary of Commerce Daniel C. Roper to form a committee to study the desirability of such unification and centralization,

---

38. Senate agreement to the conference report on H.R. 7716, February 28, 1933 (*Cong. Rec.,* 72d Cong., 2d sess., 1933, 76, pt. 5:5203–12).

39. Ibid., 5210. This exchange is part of an illuminating, much longer debate between Senators White and Dill, two of the most knowledgeable senators on the topic of communications policy.

and Roper soon convened the Interdepartmental Committee on Communications to address the issue.[40] The committee consisted of officials from several departments, including those who already had some jurisdiction over radio matters. Also included on the committee—albeit in only an advisory capacity—were the chairs of the relevant congressional subcommittees, Clarence C. Dill of the Senate Committee on Interstate Commerce and Sam Rayburn of the House Committee on Interstate and Foreign Commerce. The inclusion of members of these congressional committees was a maneuver meant to help ensure quick congressional passage of the executive committee's recommendations.

In preparing his report, Secretary Roper acknowledged that his committee was heavily influenced by the bill introduced a few years earlier by Couzens, upon which extensive hearings had been held (Stone 1991). Soon after convening, the Roper Committee issued and submitted to Roosevelt a written opinion. In this fourteen-page statement, the committee proposed the creation of a new regulatory agency, the Federal Communications Commission. Roper and his associates wrote that

> the committee recommends the transfer of existing diversified regulation of communications to a new or single regulatory body, to which would be committed any further Federal control of two-way communication and broadcasting.
>
> Although the cable, telegraph, telephone and radio are inextricably intertwined in communication, the Federal regulation of these agencies, in our country, is not centered in one governmental body. The responsibility for regulation is scattered. This scattering of the regulatory power of the Government has not been in the interest of the most economical or efficient service.[41]

The report goes on to note additional support for unification from the American Bar Association and members of the ICC, and it also lists all the benefits of such unification.[42]

While the report was clear in its recommendation of vesting responsibility for regulation in a single organization, it did not endorse either an independent commission or an executive agency as a best choice, instead arguing that either type would be acceptable so long as it regulated all

---

40. Interest groups immediately besieged the Roper Commission, which provides further evidence of the awareness that structure and process are of paramount political importance (Rosen 1980).

41. Senate Committee on Interstate Commerce, *Study of Communications by an Interdepartmental Committee,* 73d Cong., 2d sess., 1934, Senate Committee Print, 6.

42. Ibid., 7, 9.

communications. If control were given to a Cabinet officer, the report advocated the creation of a board of appeals to address issues involving equity. However, in either case it recommended that "all interested parties should have recourse to appeal to a Federal court in the District of Columbia for the purpose of appealing adverse decisions."[43]

Roosevelt quickly accepted the report and, not surprisingly, endorsed its findings.[44] In January 1934 Roosevelt transmitted to Congress his desire that such a bill be passed, along with a message voicing his support:

> I recommend that the Congress create a new agency to be known as the Federal Communications Commission, such agency to be vested with the authority now lying in the Federal Radio Commission and with such authority over communications as now lies with the Interstate Commerce Commission—the services affected to be all of those which rely on wires, cables, or radio as a medium of transmission.
>
> It is my thought that a new commission such as I suggest might be well organized this year by transferring the present authority for the control of communications of the Radio Commission and the Interstate Commerce Commission. The new body should, in addition, be given full power to investigate and study the business of existing companies and make recommendation to the Congress for additional legislation at the next session.[45]

Creating the FCC

Congress, moving quickly to act on Roosevelt's suggestion, introduced bills in each chamber on the very next day. The most important of these bills are listed in table 6.1. H.R. 8301, introduced by Representative Rayburn, was the primary bill considered in the House of Representatives. Rayburn's bill embodied Roosevelt's suggestion by proposing that the existing Radio Commission be abolished and that its functions be transferred to the new agency. Essentially, this bill supported the bringing together of the FRC and the ICC's responsibilities over telecommunica-

---

43. Ibid., 10.

44. Despite Stone's 1991 correct claim that the unification of communications regulation was not simply a New Deal invention, it seems clear that this action foreshadowed Roosevelt's proclivity to consolidate government functions. On this tendency, see Schlesinger 1958.

45. Senate, *Message from the President of the United States Recommending that Congress Create a New Agency to Be Known as the Federal Communications Commission,* 73d Cong., 2d sess., 20 February, 1934, S. Doc. 144, 1.

TABLE 6.1.   Congressional Actions on the 1934 Communications Act

House Action:
  H.R. 8301, introduced by Rayburn (D-TX)
  abolished the Radio Commission and incorporated the entire act, as amended
    —Narrow scope (questions of law)
    —Any Grants or Denials
    —D.C. Court of Appeals
    —Standing granted to anyone aggrieved by a Commission decision
    —appeals had to be filed within 20 days

Senate Action:
  S. 2910, introduced by Dill (D-WA)
    (later modified and reported as S. 3285)
  S. 2910:
    —repealed the 1927 Radio Act
    —proposed using ICC-style appeals for radio
      —appeals to district courts only
      —negative orders probably could not be appealed
      —review of questions of law only
  S. 3285:
    —refusals or grants of licenses made to the D.C. Court of Appeals
    —appeals of revocations, suspensions, or modifications to local district courts

tions into a newly created Federal Communications Commission. The radio industry was relatively pleased with this bill.

Primary attention, however, focused on bills introduced in the Senate. Despite the suggestions by Roosevelt and other legislators that the bill be written so as to minimize controversy, the first major bill introduced in this house quickly attracted attention and generated controversy. The primary concern arose from the way in which the Senate bill, S. 2910, would have gone about creating the FCC. As a first step, this bill, introduced by Senator Dill with the support of President Roosevelt, would have repealed the Radio Act of 1927. This step went far beyond anything the radio industry, or its supporters in Congress, wanted or would tolerate.[46]

The radio industry and its supporters in Congress were well aware of the implications of this act. The industry protested, arguing that Roosevelt's explicitly stated goal was to bring together regulation of different communications industries and that this goal did not imply a need to completely repeal the previous regime (*NAB Reports,* February 26, 1931). The 1927 act as amended had afforded legal security to existing radio stations,

---

46. Strangely, Roosevelt made it known that he wanted the Dill bill to become law (Friedrich and Sternberg 1943, 801).

and this security was threatened by the Dill bill's repeal of the 1927 act (Friedrich and Sternberg 1943, 802).

In large part, this legal security argument derived from the protections afforded to the industry by the judicial review provisions. As detailed in the previous chapter, the industry was very much opposed to the fact that the Dill bill's appeals provisions were drawn from the Interstate Commerce Commission's procedures.[47] Here, then, was a primary reason the industry objected to S. 2910—since the 1927 act was to be repealed, the judicial review provisions would have been similar to those written for the ICC. In particular, it implied that many agency actions that had been appealable no longer could be appealed.

Despite the avowed attempt to avoid controversy, the Senate bill was viewed by many as "drastic and novel" and was seen as "in fact an entirely new radio law" (Cushman 1941, 321).[48] According to one observer, the most drastic of its proposals were that the bill

> fixed by statute the mileage separation between high-powered stations; it reduced the licensing period for radio licenses; it permitted the commission to impose fines of $1000 per day on station owners for certain offenses; *it permitted the revocation of station licenses without a hearing; and it limited sharply the right of appeal.* (Cushman 1941, 321; emphasis added)

Because of its fear of the drastic changes implied by these proposals, industry opposition to S. 2910 was fervent. In testimony, Bellows of the NAB urged the Senate committee to amend the bill by replacing the entire radio section of S. 2910 with the portion of Rayburn's House bill that dealt with radio.[49] After additional hearings in which the NAB continued to assail the plan, the committee rewrote the bill and reintroduced it on March 28 as S. 3285.

Despite the revisions in the new version, the NAB continued to strenuously oppose Dill's bill (S. 3285), as it was reported from subcommittee, claiming that it

---

47. The ICC-style judicial review provisions also had been considered, but not adopted, at the time of the 1927 act (House 1958, 29). A convenient summary of industry objections to the provisions of S. 2910 can be found in House 1958, 29–32.

48. Dill earlier had stressed that "[a]t the present time there is no disposition to change the existing laws as they relate to broadcasting," but his bill did not match his words (*NAB Reports,* February 10, 1934).

49. See Bellows testimony in *Hearings on S. 2910,* which ended on March 9, 1934. Portions of this testimony are included in chapter 5.

has almost as many features directly injurious to broadcasting as were contained in S. 2910. Basically, the bill persists, in flat defiance of the President's clear recommendation, in legislating *before* investigation by the proposed Commission instead of *after* such investigation. (*NAB Reports,* April 7, 1934)

As an example of this problem, they cited the following:

It has an extraordinary section providing for appeals to the Court of Appeals of the District of Columbia from decisions of the proposed Commission, which makes no provision whatsoever for any appeal to this court from a decision revoking, suspending, or modifying a license. Appeals to this court would be possible only when an application is refused or granted. All other proceedings would have to be conducted before a District Court under an entirely different act. (*NAB Reports,* April 7, 1934)

The NAB therefore continued to oppose the bill on the grounds that it still was too similar to the style of judicial review that previously had been used by the Interstate Commerce Commission to review telecommunications decisions.

Several other major differences distinguished the House and Senate bills at this point. To begin with, the Senate bill was much more detailed than was the House bill. As the Senate committee wrote in its report,

In originally framing the bill two courses were open. One was to prepare a detailed and practicable bill which incorporated all legislation pertinent to the subject. The other was to draft a short bill creating the Commission and delegating to it by reference the powers now vested in the Radio Commission, the Interstate Commerce Commission, and the Postmaster General.[50]

Eventually, as acknowledged by the committee, members of the Senate chose the former route:

This bill is written as to enact the powers which the Interstate Commerce Commission and the Radio Commission now exercise over communications, by means of definite statutory provisions. This is

---

50. Senate Committee on Interstate Commerce, *Communications Act of 1934,* 73d Congress, 2d session, 17 April 1934, S. Rept. 781, 1.

preferable to leaving the Commission in doubt as to its powers by reference to general legislation primarily designed for railroads. There are certain inherent weaknesses in the present Interstate Commerce Act so far as it applies to communication companies, and these weaknesses would continue if this legislation simply transferred the powers of the Interstate Commerce Commission to this Commission. In addition certain provisions of the Radio Act are no longer applicable to radio regulation.[51]

Furthermore, the Senate specifically asked the commission to "investigate certain important phases of the communications business" and requested that it recommend amendments to the 1934 act. Finally, this bill provided that the commission be divided into two divisions—a Radio Division and a Telegraph and Telephone Division.

With respect to provisions for regulation of broadcasting, the Senate's proposal used the 1927 act as a baseline and then added many of the changes that had been proposed in H.R. 7716, the bill that President Hoover had vetoed. First, like H.R. 7716, the Senate bill allowed for appeal of certain types of orders to local district courts. As the committee noted,

> Under the Interstate Commerce Act all appeals from decisions regarding wire communications can be taken to the district courts under the three-judge court law of October 22, 1913, but appeals from decisions under the radio law can only be taken to the courts of the District of Columbia as provided in the Radio Act.
>
> This system of appeals in radio cases is extremely burdensome to owners of radio stations who live long distances from the District of Columbia. Any station owner finding it necessary to appeal from a decision of the Radio Commission must come to Washington, however great the expense for both himself and his attorney, to file and prosecute the appeal. The expenses incident to repeated trips, added to the regular legal expenses for such appeals, should not be necessary.[52]

In general, then, the Senate bill provided for ICC-style review. The committee was particularly careful to note that

> Under a number of decisions of the Supreme Court, suits to enjoin or set aside orders of the Interstate Commerce Commission as to

---

51. Ibid., 2.
52. Ibid., 9.

findings of fact can be disturbed by judicial decree only in cases where the Commission's action has been arbitrary or has transcended the legitimate bounds of the Commission's authority.[53]

At the same time, however, they acknowledged the basic differences between appeals for telephone and telegraph matters and those needed for radio. In particular, in section 402(a) they specified that when applications for new licenses were granted, refused, modified, or renewed, appeals could be taken only to the District of Columbia Court of Appeals. Other appellants, however, could appeal to the district courts.

As proposed, this section strongly favored existing stations. It specified that when a licensee wanted to appeal an action taken by the commission, it could take the appeal to the local court.[54] And in cases of new applicants, the hurdle to be cleared was set much higher—the applicant had to come to Washington, D.C., to appeal the order of the commission.[55] In its report, the committee argued that

> this appeal section is eminently fair. In nearly all cases in which the Commission makes an order affecting a licensee which the licensee did not seek, the Commission must go to the district court having jurisdiction of such licensee. Where an applicant or a licensee comes to the District of Columbia and applies for an order, he must take his appeal in the courts of the District of Columbia.[56]

The eminent fairness of this arrangement is arguable. However, what is not arguable is that this arrangement distinctly favored existing stations. Once a station was issued a license, it was spared the expense of having to return to Washington, D.C., to protest any commission action that might have affected it adversely. On the other hand, stations that were just trying to start up, and that therefore were more likely to be in a more tenuous financial situation, were forced to make the costly trip to a faraway loca-

---

53. Ibid. They argue, "By enacting this provision into this bill, the Communications Commission can rely on well-established principles of law already interpreted by the Supreme Court" (ibid.). But it also seems consistent with the idea that they did not want courts coming in with too much of a free hand and that they trusted the agency to act in their behalf.

54. "Where a licensee desires to appeal from orders of the Commission affecting his interest, but which he did not originate, he may file his appeal in the three-judge district court in the jurisdiction where he lives" (ibid.).

55. "In those cases where he has applied to the Commission for an order and desires to appeal from the Commission's action, he must come to Washington, D.C., to prosecute his appeal, just as he came to Washington to ask for the order" (ibid.).

56. Ibid., 10.

tion in order to appeal. And they did so while facing the possibility that their appeal might be in vain. The key problem for the NAB was that, as Bellows noted, a variety of decisions that the broadcasters might want to appeal would not be reviewable under these provisions. Thus, despite these other apparent factors, the NAB still wanted review of such actions and made this desire known to Congress.[57]

The House

The Senate passed S. 3285 on May 15, 1934. The bill then was forwarded to the House for consideration, where on May 21 it was referred to the Committee on Interstate and Foreign Commerce.[58] The biggest difference between the two bills continued to be that the Rayburn bill did not repeal the 1927 act but rather simply transferred the Radio Commission's duties to the new agency. Another major difference was that the House bill did not divide the commission among functional lines as sharply as did the Senate bill.

As far as review provisions are concerned, at this point there was little explicit discussion of the exact nature of how review should be structured. However, the House did acknowledge the differences between the review needed for radio and that needed for other forms of communications:

> The review now applicable to orders of the Interstate Commerce Commission will apply to suits to enforce, enjoin, set aside, annul, or suspend orders of the Communications Commission under this act, but this section will not, of course, apply in the case of matters arising in connection with the exercise of the function transferred by title III.[59]

As title III of the proposed act dealt exclusively with radio matters, it is clear that the House wanted to preserve the review provisions that had developed around the Radio Commission.

---

57. In addition, because involving the local courts would greatly increase the uncertainty of judicial outcomes, it is not clear how much of a benefit such provisions would provide.

58. Again, S. 3285 began as S. 2910. After being sent to committee, S. 2910 was modified and reported to the floor on April 19 as S. 3285. It passed, after debate and amendment, without a roll call vote.

59. House Committee on Interstate and Foreign Commerce, *Regulation of Interstate and Foreign Commerce by Wire and Radio, or for Other Purposes* 73d Cong., 2d sess., 4 June 1934, H. Rept. 1850, 7.

The Final Act

After passing the Senate on a voice vote, S. 3285 was sent to the House, where it was replaced by H.R. 8301, the Rayburn bill.[60] On June 1 the House committee reported S. 3285 to the floor, where it was amended. The bill then passed the chamber by voice vote on June 2, 1934, albeit against some serious opposition.[61] A new bill then emerged from conference and was substituted for the House and Senate bills. The conference committee bill, which "further modified the drastic proposals of the Senate" (Cushman 1941, 322), was debated in the House (but not in the Senate),[62] was passed by both houses on June 9, was signed by the president on June 14, became law on June 19, 1934 (*U.S. Statutes at Large* 48 [1934]: 1064), and went into effect on July 1, 1934.

What about the eventual provisions for judicial review? On this point, as noted, there was considerable disagreement. The eventual result was a compromise—it limited the scope of review and the venue while at the same time including a special provision to allow the district courts to review revocations. Table 5.2 presents a listing of the review provisions in the final bill.

In particular, there was disagreement within Congress over the extent of review, particularly in cases where *one* station was doing battle with the FCC, as opposed to cases where *several* stations were doing battle with each other for the initial license. Many members of Congress advocated an expansion in judicial review. These members, who for one reason or another opposed agency decision making, argued that judges should be allowed to review questions of fact (as well as questions of law) and that all federal courts should have jurisdiction. As Cass points out, "Allowing the reviewing court to examine afresh the factual issues in radio appeals obviously would lessen concerns about the agency fact-finding process" (1986, 87).

---

60. This bill was an amendment in the nature of a substitute.

61. For example, Rep. McFadden (R-PA) opposed the bill because he presciently feared that commercial stations had too much influence, and that independent stations, which lacked in political clout, would be allowed to fail, resulting in a situation where only the powerful networks remained. While the opposition was serious, it was also short, as Rayburn obtained a rule limiting debate to two hours and preventing amendments sought by opponents of commercial broadcasting.

62. Certain members of Congress refused to simply "rubber stamp a Senate bill." See Friedrich and Sternberg 1943, 803, which refers to *Congressional Record,* 73d Cong., 2d sess., 1934, 78, pt. 10:10306–32 (June 4 debate in the House of Representatives on Conf. Rep. on S. 3285). However, most of the provisions opposed by commercial broadcasters were dropped in conference, leading Bellows to crow later that "[w]hen we read it, we found out that every major point we had asked for was there" (*NAB Reports,* 15 November 1934, 618).

On the other hand, many members of Congress disagreed with this approach.[63] First of all, it raised the specter of *General Electric* types of problems. And second, many legislators actually spoke out in behalf of using an independent commission for making such regulatory decisions, emphasizing the advantages of expertise and uniform procedures.[64]

Conclusions

Several conclusions can be drawn from the discussion of Congress's role in writing the Communications Act. The first is that once again we have seen the political nature of judicial review; in the front end of the policy process, political actors pay a great deal of attention to such "details." After all, the section dealing with judicial review was among the most controversial parts of the 1934 act.

Second, an account of the path to the act's passage demonstrates that Congress is affected by the interest-group context. That is always true to some extent, of course, but it especially was true in radio during this era, given the nature of the medium. To begin with, many members saw the potential political advantage in using radio to further their political careers and were hesitant to offend the radio industry (McChesney 1994). Furthermore, because members had so little substantive understanding of the medium, they were heavily dependent on the NAB for information. And finally, the NAB was exceptionally vocal, in large part because it was so concerned about the proposal that would have repealed the 1927 act and, in so doing, would have prohibited appeal of many formerly appealable acts.

The eventual bill contained a compromise between the House, Senate, and NAB positions on the type of review that would be allowed. In particular, Congress eventually acceded to the NAB's demands that radio broadcasting be given a separate set of review provisions. While the NAB did not win every battle in Congress, it plainly was successful on a number of counts.[65]

---

63. Again, Cass: "As forcefully as these complaints were voiced, they were neither universally relevant nor unanimously endorsed. The concerns about FRC decision-making were most pressing where a proceeding pitted a single licensee against the agency, as in a license revocation. The concerns were less trenchant where the contest principally was among competitors for a license rather than between the agency and one station owner" (1989, 87).

64. See *Congressional Record*, 72d Cong., 1st sess., 1932, 75, pt. 4:3684–89 (remarks of Reps. Celler, Davis, and Lehlbach).

65. The primary battle the FCC lost was over whether the local courts would be allowed to review its decisions. On the level of NAB influence at this time, see especially the *NAB Reports* from June 16, 1934, in which the NAB boasts that it was able to substantially influence a number of sections in the Communications Act, including the section dealing with judicial review.

More than just reflecting interest-group pressures, however, Congress had its own interests in the debate over these provisions. Because there was a great deal of uncertainty about the future development of radio, Congress did not want to specify agency procedures in detail, since doing so might have left the agency unable to deal with future developments. And in an industry that was changing as rapidly as the radio industry, it was extremely likely that technological developments quickly would have overtaken the agency's ability to deal with them had Congress not left procedures fairly open.

That meant, however, that if Congress wanted to make sure that the agency did not spin out of control, it had to act to help ensure that the agency would be watched closely. Judicial review provisions were one means of accomplishing this monitoring. Again, as discussed in the previous chapter, by this time it was less obvious than it had been in 1927 that the courts were more likely to act favorably than the agency.[66] But it was still the case that members preferred at least a modicum of review. Using the concepts introduced in chapter 3, while Congress accepted the need for review, it preferred partial review (along some dimensions) to full review (along all dimensions).

Such actions reflected the institutional interests of Congress. In arguing about different types of review provisions, legislators were in effect demonstrating their concern about the overall policy impact of each potential provision. In a legal regime and institutional setting where agencies were becoming more accepted and courts somewhat less predictable, legislators were willing to give the new agency broad (some would say vague) discretionary powers. But in the end they also insisted on keeping the agency under judicial control. The legal regime played an additional role in that while some members pushed for an extremely broad standard of review, others noted that such a standard simply would not be allowed by the Supreme Court.

Once a need for judicial review was agreed upon, Congress was careful to make sure that review procedures favored existing stations—ensuring, for example, that the point of view of existing stations would be heard in court by making sure all decisions affecting these stations were appealable. These provisions, then, not only reflected the power of existing stations but also helped guarantee that the agency would not be out of control and that future developments would reflect the point of view of the stations that already had contributed to the development of the industry.

---

66. See again the quote from Senator Dill earlier in this chapter.

CHAPTER 7

Conclusions and Possibilities for Future Research

In this final chapter I have two main purposes. After recapitulating the goals and conclusions of this study, I look briefly at three court cases that took place in the aftermath of the passage of the 1934 Communications Act. The purpose of this section is straightforward—it is to see what effects the provisions for judicial review had on future court actions. Following that, I suggest some potential research projects motivated by the work done in this study.

Summary of Previous Chapters

The primary task of this project was to examine another way in which procedures and structures matter. To many scholars, this might seem to be a questionable endeavor; interest groups and members of Congress are not stupid and surely are aware that procedures matter. Yet the idea that such procedures and structures matter, that they are means by which current actors can attempt to affect future outcomes, largely has been ignored.[1] Indeed, one of the main claims of this study—that the design of judicial review is subject to political influences—has gone almost entirely unnoticed. While judicial review has been the subject of innumerable empirical and theoretical studies conducted by legal scholars and political scientists, the concept that judicial review is something that political actors think about and can affect during the front end of the policy process has gone almost completely unexplored.[2]

In earlier chapters, I used the development of regulation of broadcasting to show that the exact specification of judicial review provisions is a matter of concern to political actors. Far from being a procedural "detail" that is either given little thought or is dealt with only by those con-

---

1. See the citations in chapter 1 for a list of studies that explicitly analyze the role of structures and procedures in the calculations of political actors.

2. Again, the recent works to recognize this concept include Light 1992; Melnick 1983, 1994; and Cass 1989.

cerned with the effect of procedures on fairness or justice, judicial review provisions can be a central part of the political battles that take place during the front end of the policy process. That is, although the judiciary does not enter the process until the end of the policy game, the various players know that it will be involved and are careful to pay attention to its future role, even in the earliest stages of the policy process. While courts are reactive and will not act until called upon to review an agency action, political actors nonetheless realize that at some point courts may play a role.

A wide range of political actors are interested in these provisions. Throughout the early years of broadcast regulation, interest groups—in particular, the National Association of Broadcasters (NAB)—were broadly concerned with the specification and possible effects of these provisions. Members of Congress also paid a great deal of attention to these provisions, no doubt due (at least in part) to interest-group pressures, but more generally because the members also have preferences over outcomes and are aware that these provisions have an effect on eventual policy outcomes. Even members of the regulatory agencies expressed their preferences over judicial review.[3]

While uncovering the political nature of judicial review is an important start, this study moved beyond a simple demonstration of this point. Thus, in chapters 2 and 3, I examined a series of aspects of judicial review, unanswered theoretical questions that arise from the assertion that judicial review is not just a legal or technical detail. Why do groups and members of Congress pay attention to such procedural details? What types of provisions do these political actors choose? What affects their choices of different provisions? What factors affect their calculations of the utility of the different provisions? What factors affect the extent to which they open up agency actions to review by the judiciary?

To begin answering these questions, in chapter 2 I built on studies of the importance of bureaucratic procedures and structures. Then, working from the perspective that political actors choose such provisions strategically, I identified several different sources of information that these actors use in order to determine which provisions to choose. These actors distill information from several sources—their own substantive experience, the institutional setting, the legal regime, awareness of other interest groups—and use this information to decide which provisions to pursue. In addition, the amount of information they have about a policy area will determine the extent to which they are able to be specific about different provisions.

---

3. For example, E. O. Sykes, chair of the Federal Radio Commission, regularly testified at committee hearings about the potential effects of different sets of judicial review provisions. See, for instance, House Committee on Interstate and Foreign Commerce, *Hearings on H.R. 8301,* 73d Cong., 2d sess., 10 April 1934, 74–81.

And finally, these actors want to control the exposure of courts and agencies to different perspectives.

In chapter 3 I continued to develop a more general theory of judicial review. Using a spatial model of policy-making, I explored the conditions under which members of the enacting coalition would prefer to allow judicial review. In this chapter I also showed how judicial review can be open along some dimensions and restrained along others, and I analyzed the situations in which the coalition would prefer either full or partial review.

Central to this discussion was the concept of uncertainty. Political actors always will be uncertain about the future actions of courts and bureaucracies; yet they can also use procedures and structures to reduce this uncertainty. The amount of uncertainty, however, still will enter into their calculations. While the members of this coalition will generally prefer to vest final authority with the institution whose preferences are most similar to their own, they also will take into account uncertainty about the actions of these other institutions.

In light of the theoretical ideas set out in these two chapters, in the succeeding chapters I engaged in an empirical study of the origins of communications policy, with a special emphasis on the Communications Act of 1934 and the judicial review provisions contained therein. This act was chosen for several reasons. Communications regulation is an arena in which the courts have played a central role, making an exploration of the origins of and battles over judicial review in this area inherently interesting. Furthermore, while few sections of the 1934 act were controversial, the section containing review provisions *was* controversial. Finally, the act itself is short, as opposed to the extremely detailed regulatory statutes passed in the 1960s and 1970s. Accordingly, any findings of strategic behavior regarding review provisions is even more resonant.[4]

The Communications Act is not a perfect case; there is not always enough information about the preferences of the dominant group; there is very little information about the preferences of the weaker groups, such as educational stations, over the different provisions; and while there is a considerable record of debate within Congress, there are no roll call votes on either specific provisions or on the final act itself. Yet the evidence that does exist provides strong support for the notion that groups and members of Congress pay careful attention to the choice of these different provisions and act strategically in choosing them. While the case does not provide a complete test of all the theoretical perspectives set out earlier in this study, it does provide a test and an illustration of the main points of these theories.

---

4. Of course, the reasons for the brevity of earlier statutes may lie as much in the lack of information about these policy areas as in any sort of congressional norms toward writing legislation.

Future Consequences

As I mentioned in the previous section, regulation of communications is an area in which the actions of the courts, including the relationship between the courts and the agencies, have been extremely important over time. It therefore makes sense to explore the impact of the review provisions on later cases. While a detailed look at a number of court decisions is clearly beyond the scope of this project, a brief look at three cases should help shed light on the impact of the review provisions. These cases, three of the most well-known cases to involve the Communications Commission, are *Sanders Brothers Radio Station v. FCC*[5], *Ashbacker Radio Corporation v. FCC*,[6] and *Office of Communication of the United Church of Christ v. FCC*.[7]

Before tackling these cases, it should be stressed that the point of examining subsequent court cases is *not* to demonstrate that groups and legislators correctly predicted all the consequences of the review provisions. After all, the actual effects of judicial review provisions must be uncertain ex ante. And that is true not only of provisions for review, but for all control mechanisms, including provisions for legislative and executive influence, specification of bureaucratic processes, and specification of substantive standards.[8]

Because of the inherent uncertainty in these mechanisms, there undoubtedly will be many cases that might seem inconsistent with some of the ex ante expectations. However, what is important for legislators and interest groups in the front end of the policy process is the apparent relative advantage of mechanisms for ex post control. In the following cases, it should be kept in mind that while there were some unpredicted consequences, the review provisions generally did combine with other features of the Communications Act to increase the options for review open to station owners and to protect owners' interests.

---

5. 106 F.2d 321 (1939). While this decision was later reversed by the Supreme Court in *FCC v. Sanders Brothers Radio Station,* 309 U.S. 470 (1940), here I will concentrate on the case as heard before the Court of Appeals.

6. 326 U.S. 327 (1945).

7. 359 F.2d 994 (1966).

8. I am indebted to Ron Cass for this point. Many developments that will affect eventual political outcomes simply cannot be predicted. There is thus a similarity to chaos theory: in a complex system with many interrelated variables—such as multiple control mechanisms and several sets of actors—large patterns may be predicted, but within those patterns will be variations caused by small changes in any of these variables. See Gleick 1987.

Sanders Brothers

In May 1936, the Sanders brothers, who owned and operated radio station WKBB in East Dubuque, Illinois, applied to the Federal Communications Commission (FCC) for permission to move their transmitting apparatus to Dubuque, Iowa. Before they received approval to do so, another application for a license in the same town was received from the *Telegraph Herald,* a local Dubuque newspaper. The Sanders brothers feared that approval of the newspaper's broadcasting license would cause them economic harm, inasmuch as there would not be enough advertising revenue in the town to support both local stations. Based on this concern, the Sanders brothers decided to intervene in the *Telegraph Herald*'s proceedings.[9]

Initially, an examiner for the FCC recommended that the Sanderses' application be approved and the newspaper's be denied. Eventually, however, the commission decided to grant both licenses. The Sanders brothers quickly appealed.

The basis for their appeal was the provision of the 1934 Communications Act that allowed all parties affected by the denial *or* grant of a license to bring appeals to the Court of Appeals of the District of Columbia.[10] Under the original provisions of Section 16 of the 1927 Radio Act, it is not likely that the Sanders brothers would have been granted standing; yet under the 1934 act the question of their right to appeal was settled.

The Court of Appeals decided in favor of the Sanders brothers. In its decision, the court stressed that the FCC should have taken into account the potential economic injury to the Sanders brothers had the *Telegraph Herald*'s license been granted. The FCC had not done so, having chosen instead to grant both licenses. The appellate court, based on the Sanderses' appeal, therefore overruled the agency. Thus, the provision allowing persons other than those applying for the license to appeal resulted in a victory for the Sanders brothers.

The victory, it should be mentioned, was short-lived, as the following year the Supreme Court overruled the Court of Appeals. Still, two important points should be stressed. First, the Sanders brothers were allowed to appeal because standing for other station owners expressly was permitted by the provisions of the 1934 law. That they eventually lost their case is less important, in the context of this study, than their opportunity to press it in the first place. Because of this opportunity, they were able to—at least tem-

---

9. Parts of the account of this case rely on T. Robinson 1943 and Jameson 1979.
10. Section 402(b)(2).

porarily—overturn a commission decision that would have stood unchallenged if not for the review provisions in the Communications Act. The right to take a case to court did not guarantee existing stations the ability to have FCC decisions overturned. On the other hand, it at least increased the likelihood of such an event.

Second, the basis of the Supreme Court's ruling was that economic injury to one party should not take precedence over the public interest, since allowing it to take precedence would be profoundly anticompetitive.[11] However, it should be noted that this ruling left the door open to challenges of the grant of a license when the result of granting another license would harm the *public* by splitting available resources and causing both stations to go out of business. And, to the benefit of station owners, when the appeals court later revisited the issue, it followed this line of reasoning.

Ashbacker

The towns of Muskegon and Grand Rapids are located in the western part of central Michigan. In March 1944, the Fetzer Broadcasting Company applied to the FCC for the right to operate in Grand Rapids a new station at the frequency of 1230 kc. Shortly thereafter—and before the Fetzer application had been acted upon—the Ashbacker Radio Company filed an application to change the frequency of WKBZ, its Muskegon station, from 1490 to 1230 kc. Faced with these two applications, in June the commission ruled, without a hearing, in favor of Fetzer's application. Furthermore, it delayed action on Ashbacker's application until a later hearing could be held.[12]

At issue were what are known as "comparative hearings." The Supreme Court, in addressing Ashbacker's appeal, ruled that since the two stations were mutually exclusive (meaning that the granting of both would lead to intolerable interference), the FCC was required to hold a hearing *before* denying either application. In doing so, the Court relied on section 309(a) of the Communications Act, part of which specifies that if the commission does not find an application to be in the public interest, it must hold a hearing at which the applicant shall be provided an opportunity to be heard. The Court found this provision to be more important than another provision that gives the commission the power to grant an appli-

---

11. The Court wrote: "Plainly it is not the purpose of the Act to protect a licensee against competition but to protect the public" (*FCC v. Sanders Brothers Radio Station,* 309 U.S. 470 [1940], 475).

12. On this case, see Jameson 1979, Cass and Diver 1987, Ginsburg 1979, and especially Ulloth 1979.

cation without a hearing. The ruling therefore holds that when two applications are mutually exclusive, the right to a hearing prevails over the commission's power to grant an application without holding a hearing.

What does this case tell us? First, it demonstrates once again that an existing station was backed by the courts in its efforts to prevent a new station from encroaching on its territory. Perhaps more important, however, it demonstrates how various control mechanisms can work together. If the Communications Act contained no provision allowing losing applicants to be heard by the agency, and station owners were not allowed to seek judicial review of applications other than their own, the Court most likely would have relied on the provision allowing the commission to grant a license without a hearing. But because these provisions detailing bureaucratic and review procedures did exist together, a process was created that further advantaged existing stations.

United Church of Christ

One of the pivotal court cases of the 1960s was the case of *Office of Communication of the United Church of Christ v. FCC.*[13] This case concerned a television station, WLBT in Jackson, Mississippi, and its application for a license renewal. WLBT's recent history had not been one that most people would construe as being in the public interest. The station repeatedly had engaged in blatantly racist acts, such as when it cut away from a network program in which NAACP members were about to speak. That was not an isolated incident, either—the FCC had been receiving complaints about the actions of the station continually since 1955.

Yet despite this unsatisfactory track record, the FCC decided to grant the station's request for a license renewal. And in doing so, the agency refused to allow citizens who opposed WLBT to participate in the hearings as representatives of the listening public. The commission reasoned that

> standing is predicated upon the invasion of a legally protected interest or an injury which is direct and substantial and the "petitioners ... can assert no greater interest or claim of injury than members of the general public."[14]

Upon appeal, the Court of Appeals of the District of Columbia and then the Supreme Court overturned the agency's decision. The appellate court's decision, written by Judge Warren Burger, explicitly relied on the

---

13. The following account is drawn from Rabin 1986, Bittner 1982, and Jameson 1979.
14. 359 F.2d 994 (1966), 999.

Communications Act in its discussion of standing and its relationship to the public interest:

> The Communications Act of 1934 did not create new private rights. The purpose of the Act was to protect the public interest in communications. By section 402(b)(2), Congress gave the right of appeal to persons "aggrieved or whose interests are adversely affected" by Commission action. . . . But these private litigants have standing only as representatives of the public interest.[15]

This case demonstrates, once again, the importance of allowing standing to persons other than those directly involved in a dispute. Now it must also be recognized that this was an era in which the courts were becoming more and more lenient in granting standing, and this judicially induced expansion certainly had an effect in this case—in the past, for example, courts generally had limited grants of standing to only those who had suffered an *economic* injury.[16] Without a more lenient interpretation of standing by the courts, WLBT might have been allowed to go back on the air. But as in the *Sanders* case, the fact that a group or person other than WLBT was allowed to challenge the agency's action in court was a direct result of the provision for standing in the 1934 act.

In many ways, the main lesson here is that outcomes cannot be predicted perfectly. The case clearly shows that review provisions mattered. But in this case, the review provisions hurt, rather than helped, the existing station. The example does show that the FCC, in large part because of the other control mechanisms mentioned earlier in this chapter, was enormously biased in favor of existing stations. And it should be noted that after this case, the FCC continued to protect owners. But in this case, the review provisions hurt.

In part, the harm caused by the review provisions was due to an interesting twist. It was the specification of standing in the 1934 act that in some ways provided the logic behind the Supreme Court's loosening of requirements for standing in the 1960s.[17] Recall that Section 16 of the 1927 Radio Act did not provide the right of standing to broadcasters who were affected by decisions on licenses other than their own. In the 1934 Communications Act, this exception was redressed by providing for standing by any party aggrieved or adversely affected. And eventually, in the *Sanders* case, the Supreme Court recognized that this provision consti-

---

15. Ibid.

16. The courts *had,* however, granted standing to individual citizens in two previous cases—*Smith v. FCC,* 247 F.2d 100 (1957), and *White v. FCC,* 252 F.2d 856 (1958).

17. For more on the changes in standing, see Stewart 1975.

tuted the right of standing. The language of the Communications Act became an alternatively accepted justification for standing, along with the previously defined and recognized "legal right" test.

Once accepted by the Supreme Court in the *Sanders* case, this construction soon worked its way into other areas. Cass follows the progression of events:

> The drafters of the Administrative Procedure Act incorporated both alternatives into the APA's standing provision. Thirty years later, in its *Data Processing* decision, the Supreme Court construed the APA's Communications Act–derived alternative standing language as providing a new, generally applicable test for standing to secure judicial review of administrative action. This new test has been the basis for standing decisions that surely would have surprised any administrative lawyer of the 1930s. (1989, 95)[18]

Thus, the review provisions of the 1934 act had an effect not just on decisions within the field of communications, but also more generally. As for effects within communications, the cases cited here provide clear examples of the impact of these provisions. A systematic study of cases relating to the FCC would be illuminating in shedding further light on the impact of the review provisions in the Communications Act of 1934.[19]

Other Policy Areas

What other topics promise to be fertile ground for future exploration? In addition to the questions raised in the previous section about the relationship between the courts and the Communications Commission, one topic that arises immediately from this study is a comparative analysis of some sort. This type of study could be extended either to other policy areas or to different eras. Looking at different eras, for example, could bring out the importance of the legal regime for determining preferences. Looking at different policy areas also would provide insight into how unique aspects of different policies can affect the debates over procedural "details" and would suggest ways in which the theory could be extended and enhanced.

---

18. The case referred to in the quote is *Association of Data Processing Service Organizations, Inc. v. Camp,* 397 U.S. 150 (1970).

19. A clearly related question is how open the Communications Commission has been to review by the appellate court. This issue has been addressed frequently by scholars, especially in light of the industry's continual complaints that the courts usurped administrative authority. See Jameson 1979.

Telecommunications

One area that warrants inquiry is telecommunications policy. We have seen that one of the primary issues of contention in the debates over the 1934 Communications Act was whether radio decisions should have been covered by the review provisions that previously had been applicable to common carriers. What we have not seen, however, is that there was almost no discussion or controversy over whether those provisions should have changed for telephones. And with almost no discussion of the matter, these provisions were carried forward.

What makes this lack of controversy especially interesting is that the provisions under which ICC decisions could be reviewed originally had not been written to cover the agency's telephone decisions, but rather were the provisions in the Mann-Elkins Act designed to cover decisions regarding railroads. While telecommunications regulation technically was covered by the Mann-Elkins (1910) and Esch-Cummins (1920) bills, it was not until the Willis-Graham Act of 1921 that the debates over these acts actually included extensive discussion over the application of different provisions to telecommunications.[20] Questions thus arise about whether any discussion took place about these review provisions, and if not, why not?

Elements of the history of telecommunications regulation dovetail with the theoretical arguments made in this study. In the early 1900s, AT&T began to welcome government regulation. While it had some fear of federal regulation, this fear was tempered by the observation of the railroad industry's beneficial experience with the ICC. Institutional considerations also were salient, as regulatory agencies at the time were not especially powerful. But while an agency would not be able to control the company, it would be able to provide government approval for Bell's attempt to unify control over the phone system by purchasing other telephone companies. In addition, the legal regime was one in which the courts fiercely opposed any overreaches by agencies, while at the same time they looked favorably at consolidation of control in the telecommunications industry.[21] Allowing for regulation by agencies and judicial review by mostly sympathetic courts allowed Bell to receive official government approval for its activities while ensuring that the courts would prevent any bureaucratically imposed outcomes from deviating too far from the company's preferences.

---

20. These acts were amendments to the Interstate Commerce Act of 1887. In the case of the Esch-Cummins Act, the Senate completely ignored telecommunications, while members of the House took pains to make it clear that the changes in the act were *not* to be applicable to telecommunications. See Loeb 1978.

21. On these points, see Brock 1981, esp. 158; and MacAvoy 1965.

The Veterans Administration and the Preclusion of Review

Until recently, judicial review of benefit decisions made by the Veterans Administration (VA) had been precluded, in one form or another, since the Tucker Act of 1887.[22] In 1924, when Congress created the United States Veterans Bureau, preclusion was continued. Review again was precluded in the creation of the modern VA, by the Economy Act of 1933, and by several amendments to this act.[23]

As the word *preclusion* implies, the prohibition on judicial review of VA decisions was absolute:

> the decisions of the Administrator on any question of law or fact under any law administered by the Veterans' Administration providing benefits for veterans and their dependents or survivors shall be final and conclusive and no other official or any court of the United States shall have power or jurisdiction to review any such decision by an action in the nature of mandamus or otherwise.[24]

This absolute prohibition, although often challenged, was consistently upheld by the courts (Dale 1988; Note 1969).[25]

In 1988, however, Congress reversed decades of preclusion by passing the Veterans Judicial Review Act. A brief recounting of the path to the inclusion of judicial review provides further evidence of the political nature of judicial review. It also suggests some ways in which the theory presented in this study usefully might be extended.

The Benefits and Appeals Processes for Veterans

A detailed analysis of the process by which veterans applied for benefits is obviously beyond the scope of this study. However, a brief description of the process (as it existed from the 1930s until the late 1980s) is necessary in order to understand the significance of judicial review in this area.[26]

---

22. In this section I draw on work by Light (1992), Cogavin (1988), Rabin (1975), Note (1969), and Rashkow (1976).

23. See Cogavin 1988 for a listing of these amendments and for the best discussion of the history of judicial review of veterans benefits decisions.

24. 38 U.S.C. at 211(a) (1982).

25. An early case was *Lynch v. United States,* 292 U.S. 571 (1934). See also *Johnson v. Robison,* 415 U.S. 361 (1974). The courts did sometimes avoid construing the clause broadly, at times resulting in Congress amending the law in order to overturn the offending court decision. See *Wellman v. Whittier,* 259 F.2d 163 (D.C. Cir. 1958) and Dale 1988.

26. Most contested claims concerned either pensions or disability benefits. Here I will focus on disability benefits.

The process began with a claim, by a veteran, for benefits related to some disability connected with military service.[27] Once a veteran decided to apply for benefits, he or she filed a claim with one of the VA's field offices. A rating board, consisting of a doctor and two "rating specialists," evaluated the claim and determined eligibility. If the veteran was unhappy with the board's decision, he or she could appeal. The board had to be notified (in writing) of the appeal and then could either reopen the case or concur in its earlier opinion. If the board continued to reject the veteran's claim, it had to prepare a statement of the case, summarizing all the relevant facts and evidence. Finally, the veteran could appeal to the Board of Veterans Appeals (BVA).

Two aspects of this process merit further attention. First, if the veteran was unhappy with the decision handed down by the BVA, there was no recourse to appeal to the courts, as Section 211(a) of the law precluded any chance of judicial review. The entire process, therefore, took place within the Veterans Administration. Second, a veteran who decided to appeal a rating board's decision had three options. First, the veteran could have represented him- or herself. Second, he or she could have hired a lawyer. However, because of a Civil War statute still in effect, lawyers were not allowed to charge more than the sum total of ten dollars to represent a veteran. Needless to say, this limitation severely limited the number of lawyers who took part in this process. Third, the veteran could have received help from "military service organizations." These organizations, which included the major veterans-interest groups, such as the American Legion, the Veterans of Foreign Wars, and the Amvets, provided free assistance in the form of certified service representatives.

A veteran who sought to represent him- or herself faced several obstacles. Among the most obvious of these obstacles were a lack of knowledge about how to proceed, a lack of skill in presenting a strong case, and a lack of access to some records (which could, incidentally, be accessed by the service representatives). Since fewer than 2 percent of claimants were represented by lawyers (Rabin 1975), the obvious choice for the veteran was to enlist the help of the service representatives, who were intimately familiar with both the procedures and the personnel involved in the appeals

---

27. The connection could have been rather weak—the disability need not have occurred during military service in order for the veteran to be eligible. For example, a veteran may have had a prior condition aggravated by military service; or may have suffered an injury during service which later became debilitating; or may have suffered a disability while in the service but not active on duty.

process. And since these representatives were provided free office space in the VA headquarters, it was easy—and an obvious choice—for the veteran to enlist their services.[28]

Support for Preclusion

What was the stance on judicial review of the interested political actors? In the debates over judicial review in the 1980s (and earlier), most veterans groups, the VA, and the veterans committees in Congress firmly were opposed to ending preclusion.[29] These opponents voiced several reasons for their opposition. To begin with, they argued, the existing process was salutary, in large part because it was very informal and therefore open to veterans. Allowing for judicial review would cause the process to be formalized and judicialized, and thus more adversarial, and might cause more damage than harm. In addition, allowing for review might result in a flood of cases—many of which would have no merit—thereby burdening the courts and necessitating a significantly increased budget for the VA (to defend itself in court). Furthermore, courts did not have the specialized knowledge required to handle the cases that would come to them, and in the end very few decisions would be reversed. Most basically, the opponents argued that the process was not broken and did not need fixing.

Almost all of these objections were easily refuted. For example, the courts competently hear far more technical cases than those that would arise from VA decisions. The courts also review Social Security cases, which in many ways are similar to veterans' benefits cases. In addition, while there would be some additional costs, these costs were estimated to amount to less than .04 percent of the agency's budget (Cogavin 1988, 235).[30] Yet despite the easily refuted nature of the arguments against judicial review, for years veterans groups, satisfied with existing arrangements, were able to keep the system of preclusion in place.

---

28. Rabin describes this as "the single most distinctive characteristic of the VA process" (1975, 914). In addition to receiving office space, the groups that provided service representatives were able to use this exposure to recruit members.

29. The primary exception to this generalization was the Vietnam Veterans of America, which often took positions at odds with the other major groups (Light 1992).

30. In addition, this estimate, which amounted to an additional $12 million per year (out of a budget of $27 billion), came from the Veterans Administration, which was trying to stimulate opposition to judicial review by demonstrating its large cost. A more impartial review, issued by the Congressional Budget Office, found the costs to be roughly one-third of those cited by the VA (Cogavin 1988, 235).

Judicial Review and the Department of Veterans Affairs

Why did preclusion end in 1988? The primary cause was that a bill allowing review of veterans' benefits cases was linked to another bill, fervently supported by the VA and veterans groups, that elevated the VA to cabinet status. The Senate opponents of judicial review were able to prevent a clause allowing for judicial review from being attached to the cabinet bill, in large part because they feared that such an attachment might kill the more important cabinet bill. Proponents of review—in particular Alan Simpson (R–WY) and John Glenn (D–OH)—were, however, able to shepherd a bill allowing for judicial review through the Senate. While the two bills thus were not officially linked, proponents made it clear that the cabinet bill would be passed only if the judicial review bill was allowed to come to a vote (Light 1992).

This action left the House Veterans Committee, chaired by Sonny Montgomery (D–MS), as the last bastion of preclusion in Congress. As part of the tightest of iron triangles, this committee had long opposed judicial review. However, in 1988 it finally was forced to relent. To begin with, leaders in the Senate had managed to defeat direct linkage between the judicial review bill and the cabinet bill by promising that judicial review would be brought to the floor in the House, instead of being allowed to perish, as usual, in the Veterans Committee. House leaders thus wanted the bill to reach the floor, in part to avoid damaging the cabinet bill's chances. In addition, a large enough group of representatives, having observed the Senate's action, now favored judicial review and could credibly threaten to force the issue out of the Veterans Committee. In the end, Montgomery and his committee relented, and the Veterans Judicial Review Act of 1988 was signed into law.

Examining the Case

What does this case add to our understanding of judicial review? Most basically, it lends support to the notion that political factors affect the design of judicial review. The main veterans groups, which benefited from the existing system of internal review with no judicial appeals possible, for years had opposed all attempts to allow judicial review. They were defeated only when judicial review became tangled up in a debate over something even more important—the achievement of cabinet-level status.

This case also provides some insight into how the theory could be expanded. First of all, the case demonstrates the importance of committees within Congress. This importance was true even in the Senate, where committees play a less prominent role than they do in the House of Representatives. In the Senate, the Government Affairs Committee, which initially proposed judicial review, ran into opposition over "stealing" this issue from the Veterans Affairs Committee.[31] Jurisdictional rights clearly played a role in preventing the direct linkage between the two bills and consequently affected the final outcome.

An even more essential role in maintaining preclusion had belonged to the House Veterans Affairs Committee. Having the advantage of being in a chamber where committees play a more dominant role, this committee over the years had been able to bottle up judicial review much more tightly than had its House counterpart. The combination of the claims process and preclusion benefited the VA, which avoided judicial challenges to its decisions; it benefited the interest groups by providing them with office space and allowing them to promote their organizations to a captive audience; and it benefited the committee by giving them the continued support of the veterans groups and the VA. Indeed, the long-standing success of the House committee in preventing judicial review bills from reaching the floor demonstrates that any further examination of judicial review needs to consider the role of committees.

The case also illustrates that interest groups may oppose or favor judicial review provisions based on reasons other than due process, fairness, or legitimacy. It unequivocally shows that a group's substantive experience with an agency is important. And it shows that groups preferred the relative certainty of the existing process to the potential uncertainty of the proposed modification. But it does not address other sources of information, such as the legal climate (which was never mentioned in debates). Nor does it, for the most part, directly address either the multidimensional nature of review or whether courts could be expected to yield better outcomes, as discussed in chapter 3.[32]

What it does show is that all political benefits need not be purely policy benefits. The veterans groups clearly benefited from the preclusion of judicial review. But this benefit was *not* due to a set of decisions that helped them realize their policy goals. Indeed, most observers seemed to agree that allowing the courts to review the VA's decisions would have very lit-

---

31. On stealing jurisdiction, see D. King 1994. An exploration of the importance of committee jurisdictions in the Senate can be found in Shipan 1996.

32. However, Light (1992) presents an interesting discussion of the squabble over the scope of review and how the provision for judicial review should be worded. The House version—adopted in conference—allowed decisions to be overturned if they were "clearly erroneous," whereas the Senate version would allow decisions to be overturned only if they were "utterly lacking in a rational basis." As far as other dimensions of review are concerned, the House prevailed on creating a new Article I court (the Court of Veterans Appeals) while the Senate won on allowing a veteran to appeal the facts of his case. The differences also indicate the potential usefulness of incorporating a bicameral legislature into the theory.

tle impact on outcomes. Instead, they benefited indirectly. As nearly the only allowable advocates for veterans, they were given office space and use of other facilities at the VA. In addition, when helping veterans who were pursuing cases, they were allowed to do the equivalent of "casework" for which members of Congress are so famous. By publicizing their efforts and successes, they were able to raise money and increase their membership. And finally, they were able to keep closed the iron triangle that included the VA, the dominant veterans groups, and the veterans committees in Congress.

Remaining Theoretical Issues

Three other topics of a more theoretical nature emerge from the study and deserve to be explored. First, the model in chapter 3 could be fleshed out more carefully. In particular, as discussed earlier in this chapter, more institutional detail needs to be added to the spatial model. How does the committee system affect the design of judicial review? What happens to the results of the model if Congress is given the final word—that is, if it is allowed to react to court decisions? These types of questions need to be addressed. Relaxing some of the more severe assumptions would provide a first step toward a more realistic model.

Second, the relationship between the procedures placed on the courts and those placed on the agencies are clearly related and need to be more fully explored. Agency procedures can be thought of as ranging between two hypothetical situations—completely open (i.e., the agency has unlimited discretion) to completely closed (all actions are prescribed in minute detail in legislation). Similarly, judicial review can be either completely prohibited or allowed to an almost unlimited extent. Several questions arise regarding the relationship between these sets of provisions. Are they related? If so, how? Is it generally the case that the more open the agency procedures are, the broader judicial review must be? Or is the opposite true—do situations that call for open agency procedures also call for limited judicial review? The roles of uncertainty and information, broached at several times during this study, almost certainly would come into play here. For example, lack of information about a policy area may necessitate open agency procedures. Such procedures, however, create a great deal of uncertainty about the potential actions of the agency and consequently seem to call for at least a modicum of judicial review. These and other questions should be of interest to scholars interested in institutional politics.

Bureaucratic Drift, Legislative Drift

Finally, this type of study might provide a way to address some criticisms of earlier positive theories of the importance of structures and procedures. Shepsle, for example, while applauding the contribution of these theories, has argued that they focus too heavily on the control of bureaucratic drift while neglecting legislative drift and the related problem of time consistency.[33] Shepsle goes even further to say that there is a trade–off between legislative drift and bureaucratic drift. That is, often when members of the enacting coalition try to solve one type of drift, they end up exacerbating the other type of drift. An example would be where members of Congress construct a system in which they allow future legislators to affect bureaucratic actions. Such a system undoubtedly would reduce the problem of bureaucratic drift; at the same time, however, it also would lead to the problem of legislative drift (e.g., new members of Congress might have preferences different from those of the current members) and time inconsistency.

Another related criticism is voiced by Macey (1992b). While in an earlier article Macey (1992a) had agreed that members of the enacting coalition could use structures and procedures to increase the likelihood of certain outcomes, in this later article Macey addresses what he sees as a major shortcoming of this approach. This shortcoming is the failure to incorporate the courts into the models:

> The scholarship described above has focused extensively on the relationship between agencies and Congress; yet Congress's ability to control administrative agencies will be affected by the other branches of government. The role of these other branches in constraining or facilitating congressional control of agency decisions has not been considered. That is the goal of this article. (Macey 1992b, 674)[34]

Macey is interested primarily in the role the courts play in affecting the ability of Congress to control agencies. And the involvement of the courts, he asserts, "seriously undermines Congress's efforts to design procedural, substantive, and structural rules to control agency behavior" (1992b, 674). The primary reason is that "despite generally granting great deference to

---

33. The most explicit elaboration of this trade-off can be found in Shepsle 1992. See also Horn and Shepsle 1989; Horn 1995; Macey 1992a, 1992b; and Moe 1989, 1990a.

34. By "The scholarship described above" Macey is referring mainly to the work of McCubbins, Noll, and Weingast (1987, 1989) and his own earlier work (Macey 1992a).

agencies, the courts systematically act to broaden the array of interests with access to the administrative rulemaking process" (674).

It is arguable whether the earlier studies do indeed suffer from all the problems cited by these authors, but the criticisms do raise a number of salient questions. And it is unquestionably the case that while earlier studies by no means ignore the courts or the problem of legislative drift, they do not always place these issues at the forefront of their analyses.[35] Still, McCubbins, Noll, and Weingast offer a provocative suggestion:

> To the extent the courts pursue policy objectives that do not conform to the wishes of elected officials, administrative law (through legislation or executive order) may be in part a means for controlling the judiciary as well as for assuring adherence to democratic values. (1987, 245)

This implies that the judiciary, as well as the bureaucracy, can be subjected to procedural controls. I would suggest that this idea, as well as the work in the study presented here, supplies at least a partial answer to the criticisms of both Shepsle and Macey. While I do not propose them as definitive answers, let me suggest some related, plausible hypotheses that need to be developed and explored further.

First, it is possible to think of judicial review provisions as a means by which Congress may attempt to reduce bureaucratic drift. Shepsle contends that the main way in which bureaucratic drift can be controlled is by ensuring that the agency is susceptible to interference by future elected officials, which in turn invites the problems of legislative drift and time consistency. But adding a layer of judicial controls does not exacerbate these other problems; indeed, it keeps control out of the hands of elected officials.

Judicial review can help reduce bureaucratic drift in a number of ways. First, it can operate as the traditional model of judicial review says it should—that is, judicial review can be implemented whenever the agency oversteps the boundaries of its mandate. Second, it can subtly affect the actions of the bureaucracy even when it is not invoked. As seen in the quotation at the beginning of chapter 5, and as demonstrated in the spatial model in chapter 3, agencies are well aware of the powers of the courts to affect policy outcomes, and this awareness enters into the calculations the agency makes when reaching policy decisions. Finally, review provisions can be used to specify *which* types of actions are reviewable and

---

35. It is arguable, however, that in their concept of "autopilot" McCubbins, Noll, and Weingast do indeed address the problems of legislative drift and time consistency. See also their more explicit treatment of the courts in McNollgast 1992.

what the scope of review is, thereby opening some parts of the agency to more review and others to less. All of these strategies represent ways in which Congress can attempt to structure future outcomes and influence the agency, but *without* necessarily exacerbating problems of legislative drift or time consistency.

Macey's criticism also can be addressed by the findings of this study. It is clear that the courts can undermine some of the goals of the enacting coalition. But Macey ignores the fact that courts, too, are subject to procedural constraints, and that these constraints can be used to prevent courts from acting in ways inimical to the desires of the enacting coalition. If the enacting coalition is worried about the judiciary's definition of standing, it can specify in legislation the requirements for standing; if the coalition is worried that the courts will change a certain policy too drastically, it can make bureaucratic actions on that policy unreviewable. While this admittedly is not a foolproof method of controlling the courts, it is a plausible option that Macey ignores.

Again, the ideas in this section need to be more carefully developed. And there are certainly problems with the suggestions made here—for example, when we place a layer of court involvement on top of delegation to a bureaucracy, are we not simply replacing the problem of legislative or bureaucratic drift with "judicial drift"? But it is worth reiterating that the claims and findings of this study can at least partially address the criticisms of Shepsle and Macey. Putting the courts in place to review the agencies is a way in which the enacting coalition can try to minimize bureaucratic drift without at the same time increasing the chances of legislative drift. And once the courts are put in place, they, too, are subject to carefully considered procedural constraints.

Looking Ahead

All these topics, both the empirical and the theoretical ones, present potentially worthwhile research opportunities. And all are consistent with the work done in this study. As we have seen, scholars have begun to make significant strides toward a better understanding of institutions and institutional design. This study has added to the growing literature on institutions by addressing the question of how political actors think about the courts. This results of this study, along with the suggestions for future research, hopefully have carried us farther toward a more complete understanding of institutions and, in particular, of judicial review.

Appendixes

Appendix A

First, let us again assume a two-dimensional space and Euclidean preferences. Because the outcome will be determined in part by the location of the status quo, we need to decide how to map out the policy space in a systematic manner. It turns out that with the courts functioning as a policy gatekeeper in two-dimensional space, q can be located in sixteen different regions. Figure 3.3 demonstrates that by using three vertical lines ($y1$, $y2$, and $y3$) and three horizontal lines ($x1$, $x2$, and $x3$) to divide the policy space.[1]

The judiciary's ability to determine whether to overrule the agency, where such an action will lead to a return to the status quo, again adds an element of strategy to this game. More specifically, it means that even the *possibility* of judicial review will affect the agency's decision, causing the agency to choose its policy while strategically keeping the judiciary's preferences in mind. That is, the agency, taking into account the location of the judiciary and the status quo, will propose a policy that produces the best outcome it can achieve.

As an example, if the status quo q is located in region 10, then it would be foolish for the agency to propose A, since the judiciary would (if allowed by the law) simply overrule the agency along both dimensions, resulting in a policy outcome of q.[2] Instead, the agency can act strategically and choose a point, z, located between A and J, that is the same distance from J as is q (i.e., $|J - z| = |J - q|$). This proposal obviously is not as good for the agency as is point A, but it is clearly better along both dimensions than is q. Since the judiciary is indifferent between q and z, it will not

---

1. Two of the lines—$y2$ and $x2$—are the lines passing through J. Two other lines—$y3$ and $x1$—are similarly drawn through A. Finally, $y1$ is drawn parallel to $y3$ such that any time a vertical line (such as $x1$) intersects these two lines, J is indifferent between the points of intersection. For example, along $x2$, J is indifferent between $y1$ and $y3$. The line $x3$ represents a similar set of points along the other dimension. This plotting leads to the sixteen separate regions in which the status quo can exist. This figure may seem unnecessarily messy, but it is complete; and again, a status quo in each region may produce a different outcome.

2. For the sake of this example, assume that $C = J$. The importance of the location of C will be taken up after first detailing the outcomes that could result under different types of review.

overrule the agency. The agency, through a strategic proposal, has ended up much better off than if it behaved sincerely.

What will the agency do if q is in, say, region 2? To begin with, it knows that it does not need to worry about being overturned along the vertical dimension, as it is closer to J along this dimension than is q. However, it also knows that along the horizontal dimension the judiciary prefers q to A. Thus the agency will locate along $x1$ at a point as far to the right of J as q is to the left.

The agency can engage in this type of behavior no matter where the status quo is located. The key determinants of the agency's choices are the locations of A, J, and q, where q can exist in any of the sixteen regions seen in figure 3.3. In each case, the agency will choose the policy that it most favors and that also will not be overturned by the judiciary. Table A.1 lists the outcomes, given full review, resulting from all sixteen possible status quo locations.

Choosing Review

Now, as argued earlier, Congress (or an interest group) is predominantly interested in the eventual policy outcome, and not merely in which institution has the authority to make the final decision. Congress will want to

TABLE A.1.   Location of Outcomes under Full Review

Location of Status Quo	Outcome with Full Review
1	A
2	$x1$ border at $2J_x - q_x$
3	projection of q on $x1$
4	A
5	projection of q on $y3$
6	$2J_x - q_x$ along a horizontal line through q
7	q
8	projection of q on $y3$
9	$y3$ border at $2J_y - q_y$
10	Inside 7 at $2J_{x,y} - q_{x,y}$
11	$2J_y - q_y$ along a vertical line through q
12	$y3$ border at $2J_y - q_y$
13	A
14	$x1$ border at $2J_x - q_x$
15	projection of q on $x1$
16	A

Note: All outcomes are in or on the border of region 7. Thus, "$x1$ border at $2J_x - q_x$" means the outcome is along the $x1$ border of region 7 at a point as far to the right of J as q is to the left of J. "Projection of q on $x1$" is the point at which a line drawn through q and perpendicular to $x1$ intersects $x1$.

vest final authority in the institution that promises to produce the most favorable outcome, which means that Congress also will take care to choose the *type* of review that will yield the best possible outcome. In other words, in some cases Congress will prefer to have full review, in other cases it will prefer to have partial (either horizontal or vertical) review, and in still other cases it will prefer to have no review at all. Table A.2 presents a list of all of the possible outcomes given each type of review. An important point to notice here is that *all* outcomes are either in or along the border of region 7.

Overall, what will Congress prefer? The answer is not as straightforward as it was when the judiciary was treated as a policy selector. Let us begin by talking about the easier cases.

First, what if Congress is located in regions 1 or 2? In this case, Congress will prefer horizontal review. That makes sense, as Congress would not mind the court moving the agency's policy to the left but also would not want the policy to be lowered at all. More systematically, let us go back to table A.2. First, without any review at all, the outcome will always be A. Second, horizontal review always gives an outcome along the $x1$ border of region 7 or at A, whereas vertical review yields outcomes either at A

TABLE A.2.   List of Outcomes under Full and Partial Review

Location of Status Quo	Full Review	Partial Review	
		Horizontal	Vertical
1	A	A	A
2	$x1$ border	$x1$ border	A
3	$x1$ border	$x1$ border	A
4	A	A	A
5	$y3$ border	A	$y3$ border
6	Inside 7	$x1$ border	$y3$ border
7	Inside 7	$x1$ border	$y3$ border
8	$y3$ border	A	$y3$ border
9	$y3$ border	A	$y3$ border
10	Inside 7	$x1$ border	$y3$ border
11	Inside 7	$x1$ border	$y3$ border
12	$y3$ border	A	$y3$ border
13	A	A	A
14	$x1$ border	$x1$ border	A
15	$x1$ border	$x1$ border	A
16	A	A	A

Note: An outcome of "$x1$ border" designates that the outcome will be along the segment of $x1$ that forms the border of region 7; similarly, "$y3$ border" designates that the outcome will be along the segment of $y3$ that forms the border of region 7. For a more specific description of the locations, see table A.1.

or along the $y3$ border of region 7. Now if Congress is in regions 1 or 2, it will prefer any point along the $x1$ border of region 7 to A, and therefore horizontal review to no review. Similarly, a Congress located in these regions will prefer A to any point along the $y3$ border of region 7 and, by transitivity, will prefer any point along the $x1$ border to any point along the $y3$ border. In these cases, Congress will clearly prefer horizontal review to either no review or vertical review.[3]

Will a Congress located in regions 1 or 2 prefer horizontal review to full review? In half the cases (when the status quo is located in regions 1 through 4 or 13 through 16), the outcomes are the same. And for some status quo locations—regions 5, 8, 9, and 12—horizontal review is clearly preferred. In the other cases, however, the outcomes can be mixed. For example, would a Congress located in region 6 prefer an outcome along the $x1$ border or one inside region 7? There are clearly points in the interior of region 7 that are preferable to points along the $x1$ border. But on average Congress will prefer a lottery of points along the $x1$ border to a lottery of points contained within the interior of region 7. And Congress therefore will prefer to give the judiciary the power to review only the horizontal component of the agency's decision.

If Congress is located in regions 12 or 16, the logic is similar. Overall, Congress will prefer to vest the court with partial review—this time with vertical review, as Congress prefers the vertical component of the court's location to the vertical component of the agency's location. Congress prefers any point along the $y3$ border to A and prefers A to any point along the $x1$ border. A glance at table A.2 confirms that Congress prefers vertical review to the other options.[4]

Next, what about the case in which Congress is located in region 4? In this case, it will prefer no review at all. In the absence of review, the outcome will be A. From figure 3.3 we can see that if Congress is located in region 4, it will prefer A to any point in or on the border of region 7. Since all types of review yield some outcomes in or on the border of region 7, Congress will prefer to prevent any kind of review.

---

3. Table A3.2 shows that from Congress's perspective, horizontal review is an improvement over no review in half the cases, provides the same outcome in the other half, and therefore is preferred. Horizontal review also provides an outcome as good as or better than vertical review in all cases. In some cases it yields the same outcome (A). In other cases it produces an outcome on the $x1$ border, whereas vertical review results in an outcome either at A or along the $y3$ border, or it yields an outcome of A, whereas vertical review yields an outcome on the $y3$ border.

4. For example, Congress is indifferent between full and vertical review if the status quo lies in regions 1, 4, 5, 8, 9, 12, 13, or 16; always prefers vertical review if the status quo lies in regions 2, 3, 14, or 15; and prefers vertical review, on average, if q is in regions 6, 7, 10, or 11. Overall, therefore, it prefers vertical review to full review.

What if Congress is located below $x2$ and to the left of $y2$ (regions 9, 10, 13, 14)? In this case, it will clearly prefer full review. The effect of full review is to draw outcomes away from A and closer to J. As seen in table A.2, all the outcomes with full review will be at least as good as, and often better than, the outcomes with either partial review or no review.

These have been the straightforward cases. If Congress is located in any of the regions not divided by dotted lines, its decision is clear—Congress will decide to vest final authority in the institution to which it is closest and will do so along each dimension. However, there are other points in this policy space where Congress is definitely closer to one or the other institution but where the decision is not so clear. These regions of uncertainty are all the regions that contain dotted lines.

What will happen if Congress is in, say, region 5 or 6? If C is located below the dotted line, it will prefer full review, as table A.2 shows that this style of review pulls the outcome closest to these areas. A similar result obtains for the other regions in the lower left quadrant. For the other parts of regions 5, 6, 11, and 15, the result depends on the location of q. Except in situations where q is located between A and $C(A)$ (see note 14 to chapter 3), Congress will choose to prevent judicial review in the dimension where it is closer to A. Equivalent results hold for the rest of the figure. Congress will prefer to allow judicial review whenever it is closer to the judiciary along a given dimension; and in most cases, it will limit judicial review when it is closer to the agency. But in every case, it can manipulate outcomes by strategically selecting the type of review.

Appendix B

Section 16 of the Radio Act of 1927 provides as follows:

Any applicant for a construction permit, for a station license, or for the renewal or modification of an existing station license whose application is refused by the licensing authority shall have the right to appeal from said decision to the Court of Appeals of the District of Columbia; and any licensee whose license is revoked by the commission shall have the right to appeal from such decision of revocation to said Court of Appeals of the District of Columbia or to the district court of the United States in which the apparatus licensed is operated, by filing with said court, within twenty days after the decision complained of is effective, notice in writing of said appeal and of the reasons therefor.

The licensing authority from whose decision an appeal is taken shall be notified of said appeal by service upon it, prior to the filing thereof, of a certified copy of said appeal and of the reasons therefor. Within twenty days after the filing of said appeal the licensing authority shall file with the court the originals or certified copies of all papers and evidence presented to it upon the original application for a permit or license or in the hearing upon said order of revocation, and also a like copy of its decision thereon and a full statement in writing of the facts and the grounds for its decision as found and given by it. Within twenty days after the filing of said statement by the licensing authority either party may give notice to the court of his desire to adduce additional evidence. Said notice shall be in the form of a verified petition stating the nature and character of said additional evidence, and the court may thereupon order such evidence to be taken in such manner and upon such terms and conditions as it may deem proper.

At the earliest convenient time the court shall hear, review, and determine the appeal upon said record and evidence, and may alter or revise the decision appealed from and enter such judgement as to it may seem just. The revision by the court shall be confined to the points set forth in the reasons of appeal.

References

Aberbach, Joel. 1990. *Keeping a Watchful Eye.* Washington, DC: Brookings Institution.

American Bar Association. 1927. "Report of the Standing Committee on Air Law." *American Bar Association Reports* 52:232–35.

Arnold, R. Douglas. 1990. *The Logic of Congressional Action.* New Haven: Yale University Press.

Austen-Smith, David, and John R. Wright. 1994. "Counteractive Lobbying." *American Journal of Political Science* 38 (1): 25–44.

Barnouw, Eric. 1966. *A Tower in Babel: A History of Broadcasting in the United States, Volume I—to 1933.* New York: Oxford University Press.

———. 1968. *The Golden Web: A History of Broadcasting in the United States, Volume II, 1933–1953.* New York: Oxford University Press.

Bauer, Raymond A., Ithiel de Sola Pool, and Lewis Anthony Dexter. 1972. *American Business and Public Policy,* 2d ed. New York: Adline Publishing Co.

Bawn, Kathleen. 1995. "Political Control versus Expertise: Congressional Choice about Administrative Procedures." *American Political Science Review* 89 (1): 62–73.

Bawn, Kathleen, and Charles R. Shipan. 1993. "Congressional Responses to Supreme Court Decisions: An Institutional Perspective." Paper presented at the annual meeting of the American Political Science Association, Washington, DC, September 1–5.

Bentley, Arthur. 1908. *The Process of Government.* Chicago: University of Chicago Press.

Berman, Manuel K. 1933. "Regulation of Radio Broadcasting." *Boston University Law Review* 13:60–73.

Berry, Donald A., and Bernard W. Lindgren. 1990. *Statistics: Theory and Methods.* Pacific Grove, CA: Brooks/Cole Publishing.

Berry, Tyler. 1937. *Communications by Wire and Radio.* Chicago: Callaghan and Co.

Bittner, John R. 1982. *Broadcast Law and Regulation.* Englewood Cliffs, NJ: Prentice-Hall.

The Broadcasting Yearbook. 1939. Washington, DC: Broadcasting Publications.

Brock, Gerald W. 1981. *The Telecommunications Industry: The Dynamics of Market Structure.* Cambridge: Harvard University Press.

Caldeira, Gregory A., and John R. Wright. 1988. "Interest Groups and Agenda

Setting in the Supreme Court of the United States." *American Political Science Review* 82:1109–1127.

Caldwell, Louis G. 1930. "Appeals from Decisions of the Federal Radio Commission." *Journal of Air Law* 1:274–320.

Cameron, Charles M. 1993. "New Avenues for Modeling Judicial Politics." Paper presented at the Conference on the Political Economy of Public Law, University of Rochester, October 15–16.

Cameron, Charles M., Albert D. Cover, and Jeffrey A. Segal. 1990. "Senate Voting on Supreme Court Nominees." *American Political Science Review* 84:525–34.

Cameron, Charles M., Jeffrey A. Segal, and Albert D. Cover. 1995. "Signals and Indices in the Supreme Court's Certiorari Decisions." Paper presented at the annual meeting of the Midwest Political Science Association, Chicago, April 6–9.

Carter, Lief H., and Christine B. Harrington. 1991. *Administrative Law and Politics,* 2d ed. New York: Harper Collins.

Cass, Ronald A. 1986. "Models of Administrative Action." *Virginia Law Review* 72 (2): 363–98.

———. 1989. "Review, Enforcement, and Power under the Communications Act of 1934: Choice and Chance in Institutional Design." In *A Legislative History of the Communications Act of 1934,* ed. Max D. Paglin. New York: Oxford University Press.

Cass, Ronald A., and Colin S. Diver. 1987. *Administrative Law: Cases and Methods.* Boston: Little Brown and Co.

Choper, Jesse H. 1980. *Judicial Review and the National Political Process: A Functional Reconsideration of the Role of the Supreme Court.* Chicago: University of Chicago Press.

Clinton, Robert Lowry. 1989. *Marbury v. Madison and Judicial Review.* Lawrence: University of Kansas.

Coase, Ronald A. 1959. "The Federal Communications Commission." *Journal of Law and Economics* 2 (October): 1–40.

Cogavin, Mary. 1988. "The Case for Judicial Review of Veterans' Administration Benefit Determinations." *Administrative Law Journal* 2:217–41.

Corwin, Edward S. 1934. *The Twilight of the Supreme Court.* New Haven: Yale University Press.

Couzens, James. 1930. "A Commission on Communications." In *Radio and its Future,* ed. Martin Codel. New York: Harper and Bros. Publishers.

Cushman, Robert E. 1941. *The Independent Regulatory Commissions.* New York: Oxford University Press.

Dahl, Robert A. 1957. "Decision-Making in a Democracy: The Supreme Court as a National Policy-Maker." *Journal of Public Law* 6:279–95.

Dale, Charles V. 1988. "Statutory Preclusion of Veterans' Claims from Judicial Review under 38 U.S.C. 211(a)." CRS Report for Congress, May 11. Washington, DC: Library of Congress.

Davies, Joseph E. 1923. "The Federal Trade Commission." In *The Growth of American Administrative Law.* St. Louis: Thomas Law Book Co.

Davis, Frederick. 1964. "Veterans' Benefits, Judicial Review, and the Constitutional Problems of 'Positive' Government." *Indiana Law Journal* 39 (2): 183–227.

Dill, Clarence C. 1970. *Where Water Falls.* Spokane, WA: Clarence C. Dill.

Douglas, George H. 1987. *The Early Days of Radio Broadcasting.* Jefferson, NC: McFarland and Co.

Edelman, Murray. 1950. *The Licensing of Radio Services in the United States, 1927–1947.* Urbana: University of Illinois Press.

Ely, John Hart. 1980. *Democracy and Distrust: A Theory of Judicial Review.* Cambridge: Harvard University Press.

Eoyang, Thomas T. 1936. *An Economic Study of the Radio Industry in the United States of America.* New York: Columbia University Press.

Epstein, David, and Sharyn O'Halloran. 1994. "Administrative Procedures, Information, and Agency Discretion." *American Journal of Political Science* 38:697–722.

Epstein, Lee. 1985. *Conservatives in Court.* Knoxville: University of Tennessee Press.

———. 1991. "Courts and Interest Groups." In *The Courts: A Critical Assessment,* ed. John B. Gates and Charles A. Johnson. Washington, DC: CQ Press.

Epstein, Lee, and Jack Knight. 1995. "Documenting Strategic Interaction on the U.S. Supreme Court." Paper presented at the annual meeting of the American Political Science Association, Chicago, August 30–September 3.

Eskridge, William N., Jr. 1991a. "Reneging on History? Playing the Court/Congress/President Civil Rights Game." *California Law Review* 79 (3): 613–84.

———. 1991b. "Overriding Supreme Court Statutory Interpretation Decisions." *Yale Law Journal* 101 (2): 331–455.

Eskridge, William N., Jr., and John A. Ferejohn. 1992. "The Article I, Section 7 Game." *Georgetown Law Journal* 80 (3): 523–64.

———. 1994. "Politics, Interpretation, and the Rule of Law." *NOMOS* 36:265–94.

Fainsod, Merle, and Lincoln Gordon. 1941. *Government and the American Economy.* New York: W.W. Norton and Co.

Farber, Daniel A., and Philip P. Frickey. 1988. "Legislative Intent and Public Choice." *Virginia Law Review* 74 (2): 423–69.

———. 1991. *Law and Public Choice: A Critical Introduction.* Chicago: University of Chicago Press.

Federal Radio Commission. 1928. *United States Federal Radio Commission Annual Report,* vol. 2. Washington, DC: United States Government Printing Office.

Ferejohn, John, and Charles R. Shipan. 1988. "Congressional Influence on Telecommunications Policy." Paper presented at the Center for Economic Policy Research Conference on Telecommunications, Stanford University, March.

———. 1989. "Congressional Influence on Administrative Agencies: A Case Study of Telecommunications Policy." In *Congress Reconsidered,* 4th ed., ed. Lawrence C. Dodd and Bruce I. Oppenheimer. Washington, DC: CQ Press.

———. 1990. "Congressional Influence on Bureaucracy." *Journal of Law, Economics, and Organization* 6:1–20.

Ferejohn, John A., and Barry R. Weingast. 1992. "Limitation of Statutes: Strategic Statutory Interpretation." *Georgetown Law Journal* 80 (3): 565–82.

Fiorina, Morris P. 1982. "Legislative Choice of Regulatory Forms: Legal Process or Administrative Process?" *Public Choice* 39:33–66.

———. 1985. "Group Concentration and the Delegation of Legislative Authority." In *Regulatory Policy and the Social Sciences,* ed. Roger G. Noll. Berkeley: University of California Press.

———. 1986. "Legislator Uncertainty, Legislative Control, and the Delegation of Legislative Power." *Journal of Law, Economics, and Organization* 2:33–51.

Fisher, William W. 1991. "The Development of Modern American Legal Theory and the Judicial Interpretation of the Bill of Rights." In *A Culture of Rights,* ed. Michael J. Lacey and Knud Haakonssen. New York: Cambridge University Press.

Fletcher, Robert V. 1923. "The Interstate Commerce Commission." In *The Growth of American Administrative Law,* ed. Ernst Freund. St. Louis: Thomas Law Book Co.

Friedrich, Carl J., and Evelyn Sternberg. 1943. "Congress and the Control of Radio-Broadcasting." *American Political Science Review* 37 (5): 797–818.

Gely, Rafael, and Pablo T. Spiller. 1990. "A Rational Choice Theory of Supreme Court Decision Making with Applications to the *State Farm* and *Grove City* Cases." *Journal of Law, Economics, and Organization* 6:263–300.

George, Alexander. 1979. "Case Studies and Theory Development: The Method of Structured, Focused Comparison." In *Diplomacy: New Approaches in History, Theory, and Policy,* ed. Paul Gordon Lauren. New York: Free Press.

George, Tracey E., and Lee Epstein. 1992. "On the Nature of Supreme Court Decision Making." *American Political Science Review* 86 (2): 323–37.

Gilligan, Thomas W., and Keith Krehbiel. 1989. "Asymmetric Information and Legislative Rules with a Heterogenous Committee." *American Journal of Political Science* 33:459–90.

———. 1990. "Organization of Informational Committees by a Rational Legislature." *American Journal of Political Science* 34:531–64.

Ginsburg, Douglas H. 1979. *Regulation of Broadcasting: Law and Policy Towards Radio, Telecommunications, and Cable Communications.* St. Paul, MN: West Publishing Co.

Gleick, James. 1987. *Chaos: Making a New Science.* New York: Viking Press.

Glick, Henry R. 1988. *Courts, Politics, and Justice,* 2d ed. New York: McGraw-Hill.

Hayes, Michael T. 1981. *Lobbyists and Legislators: A Theory of Political Markets.* New Brunswick, NJ: Rutgers University Press.

Hazlett, Thomas W. 1990. "The Rationality of U.S. Regulation of the Broadcast Spectrum." *Journal of Law and Economics* 33 (April): 133–75.

Head, Sydney W. 1976. *Broadcasting in America,* 3d ed. Boston: Houghton Mifflin.

Heclo, Hugh. 1989. "American Politics Remade." In *Remaking American Politics,* ed. Richard A. Harris and Stanley M. Milkis. Boulder, CO: Westview Press.

Herring, E. Pendleton. 1936. *Public Administration and the Public Interest.* New York: McGraw-Hill.

Herring, James M., and Gerald C. Gross. 1936. *Telecommunications, Economics, and Regulation.* New York: McGraw-Hill.

Hill, Jeffrey S., and James E. Brazier. 1991. "Constraining Administrative Decisions: A Critical Examination of the Structure and Process Hypothesis." *Journal of Law, Economics, and Organization* 7:373–400.

Horn, Murray J. 1995. *The Political Economy of Public Administration.* New York: Cambridge University Press.

Horn, Murray J., and Kenneth A. Shepsle. 1989. "Commentary on 'Administrative Arrangements and the Political Control of Agencies': Administrative Process and Organizational Form as Legislative Responses to Agency Costs." *Virginia Law Review* 75:499–508.

Huntington, Samuel P. 1953. "The Marasmus of the ICC." *Yale Law Journal* 61 (April): 467–508.

Ignagni, Joseph, and James Meernik. 1994. "Explaining Congressional Attempt to Reverse Supreme Court Decisions." *Political Research Quarterly* 47 (June): 353–71.

Inglis, Andrew F. 1990. *Behind the Tube: A History of Broadcasting Technology and Business.* Boston: Focal Press.

Jackson, Robert H. 1941. *The Struggle for Judicial Supremacy.* New York: Alfred A. Knopf.

Jaffe, Louis L. 1965. *Judicial Control of Administrative Action* (abridged student edition). Boston: Little, Brown.

Jameson, Kay Charles. 1979. *The Influence of the United States Court of Appeals for the District of Columbia on Federal Policy in Broadcast Regulation, 1929–1971.* New York: Arno Press.

Karlan, Pamela S., and Peyton McCrary. 1988. "Book Review: Without Fear and Without Research: Abigail Thernstrom on the Voting Rights Act." *Journal of Law and Politics* 4:751–77.

Katzmann, Robert A. 1980. "Federal Trade Commission." In *The Politics of Regulation,* ed. James Q. Wilson. New York: Basic Books.

———. 1986. *Institutional Disability: The Saga of Transportation Policy for the Disabled.* Washington, DC: Brookings Institution.

———. 1988. *Judges and Legislators: Toward Institutional Comity.* Washington, DC: Brookings Institution.

———. 1992. "Bridging the Statutory Gulf Between Courts and Congress: A Challenge for Positive Political Theory." *Georgetown Law Review* 80 (3): 653–69.

King, David C. 1994. "On the Nature of Congressional Committee Jurisdictions." *American Political Science Review* 88:48–63.

King, Gary, Robert O. Keohane, and Sidney Verba. 1994. *Designing Social Inquiry.* Princeton: Princeton University Press.

Knott, Jack H., and Gary J. Miller. 1987. *Reforming Bureaucracy: The Politics of Institutional Choice.* Englewood Cliffs, NJ: Prentice-Hall.

Krasnow, Erwin G., Lawrence E. Longley, and Herbert A. Terry. 1982. *The Politics of Broadcast Regulation,* 3d ed. New York: St. Martin's Press.

Krehbiel, Keith. 1991. *Information and Legislative Organization.* Ann Arbor: University of Michigan Press.

Landes, William, and Richard A. Posner. 1975. "The Independent Judiciary in an Interest Group Perspective." *Journal of Law and Economics* 18:875–911.

Landis, James M. 1938. *The Administrative Process.* New Haven: Yale University Press.

Lasser, William. 1988. *The Limits of Judicial Power.* Chapel Hill: University of North Carolina Press.

Latham, Earl. 1952. *The Group Basis of Politics.* Ithaca, NY: Cornell University Press.

Leblebici, Huseyin, Gerald R. Salancik, Anne Copay, and Tom King. 1991. "Institutional Chance and the Transformation of Interorganizational Fields: An Organizational History of the U.S. Radio Broadcasting Industry." *Administrative Science Quarterly* 36:333–63.

Le Duc, Don R., and Thomas A. McCain. 1970. "The Federal Radio Commission in Federal Court: Origins of Broadcast Regulatory Doctrines." *Journal of Broadcasting* 14 (4): 393–410.

Light, Paul C. 1992. *Forging Legislation.* New York: W.W. Norton and Co.

Loeb, G. Hamilton. 1978. "The Communications Act Policy Toward Competition: A Failure to Communicate." *Duke Law Journal* 1978 (March): 1–56.

Maass, Arthur. 1983. *Congress and the Common Good.* New York: Basic Books.

MacAvoy, Paul W. 1965. *The Economic Effects of Regulation: The Trunkline Railroad Cartels and the Interstate Commerce Commission Before 1900.* Cambridge: MIT Press.

Macey, Jonathan R. 1992a. "Organizational Design and Political Control of Administrative Agencies." *Journal of Law, Economics, and Organization* 8:93–110.

———. 1992b. "Separated Powers and Positive Political Theory: The Tug of War Over Administrative Agencies." *Georgetown Law Journal* 80 (3): 671–703.

March, James G., and Johan P. Olsen. 1989. *Rediscovering Institutions.* New York: Free Press.

Marks, Brian A. 1988. "A Model of Judicial Influence on Congressional Policymaking: *Grove City College v. Bell.*" Working paper in political science, the Hoover Institution, Stanford University.

Mashaw, Jerry L. 1985. "Prodelegation: Why Administrators Should Make Political Decisions." *Journal of Law, Economics, and Organization* 1:81–100.

———. 1990. "Explaining Administrative Process: Normative, Positive, and Critical Stories of Legal Development." *Journal of Law, Economics, and Organization* 6:267–98.

McChesney, Robert W. 1994. *Telecommunications, Mass Media, and Democracy: The Battle for the Control of U.S. Broadcasting, 1928–1935.* New York: Oxford University Press.

McCubbins, Mathew D. 1985. "Legislative Design of Regulatory Structure." *American Journal of Political Science* 29:721–48.

McCubbins, Mathew D., Roger G. Noll, and Barry R. Weingast. 1987. "Administrative Procedures as Instruments of Political Control." *Journal of Law, Economics, and Organization* 3:243–77.

———. 1989. "Structure and Process, Politics and Policy: Administrative Arrangements and the Political Control of Agencies." *Virginia Law Review* 75:431–82.

McCubbins, Mathew D., and Talbot Page. 1987. "A Theory of Congressional Delegation." In *Congress: Structure and Policy*, ed. Mathew D. McCubbins and Terry Sullivan. Cambridge: Cambridge University Press.

McFarland, Carl. 1933. *Judicial Control of the Federal Trade Commission and the Interstate Commerce Commission, 1920–1930*. Cambridge: Harvard University Press.

McNollgast. 1992. "Positive Canons: The Role of Legislative Bargains in Statutory Interpretation." *Georgetown Law Journal* 80 (3): 705–42.

Melnick, R. Shep. 1983. *Regulation and the Courts*. Washington, DC: Brookings Institution.

———. 1985. "The Politics of Partnership." *Public Administration Review*. 45:653–60.

———. 1989. "The Courts, Congress, and Programmatic Rights." In *Remaking American Politics*, ed. Richard A. Harris and Stanley M. Milkis. Boulder, CO: Westview Press.

———. 1994. *Between the Lines*. Washington, DC: Brookings Institution.

Mensch, Elizabeth. 1990. "The History of Mainstream Legal Thought." In *The Politics of Law: A Progressive Critique*, ed. David Kairys. New York: Pantheon Books.

Miller, Mark C. 1990. "Federal Court Decisions versus Federal Agency Decisions: How Congressional Committees Differ in Their Reactions." Paper presented at the annual meeting of the American Political Science Association, San Francisco, August 30–September 2.

———. 1992. "Congressional Committees and the Federal Courts: A Neo-institutional Perspective." *Western Political Quarterly* 45:949–70.

Minasian, Jora R. 1969. "The Political Economy of Broadcasting in the 1920's." *Journal of Law and Economics* 12:391–403.

Moe, Terry M. 1989. "The Politics of Bureaucratic Structure." In *Can the Government Govern?*, ed. John E. Chubb and Paul E. Peterson. Washington, DC: Brookings Institution.

———. 1990a. "The Politics of Structural Choice: Toward a Theory of Public Bureaucracy." In *Organization Theory: From Chester Barnard to the Present and Beyond*, ed. Oliver E. Williamson. New York: Oxford University Press.

———. 1990b. "Political Institutions: The Neglected Side of the Story." *Journal of Law, Economics, and Organization* 6:213–53.

Murphy, Walter F. 1962. *Congress and the Court*. Chicago: University of Chicago Press.

———. 1964. *Elements of Judicial Strategy*. Chicago: University of Chicago Press.

Noll, Roger G., and Haruo Shimada. 1991. "Political Responses to Economic Dislocations." In *Parallel Politics,* ed. Samuel Kernell. Washington, DC: Brookings Institution.

Nordhaus, R. J. 1932. "Judicial Control of the Federal Radio Commission." *Journal of Radio Law* 2 (3): 447–72.

Note. 1934. "Communications Act of 1934." *Virginia Law Review* 21:318–25.

———. 1969. "Judicial Review and the Governmental Recovery of Veterans' Benefits." *University of Pennsylvania Law Review* 118:288–98.

———. 1982. "'Round and 'Round the Bramble Bush: From Legal Realism to Critical Legal Scholarship." *Harvard Law Review* 95:1669–90.

O'Connor, Karen. 1980. *Women's Organizations' Use of the Court.* Lexington, MA: Lexington Books.

Olson, Mancur, Jr. 1965. *The Logic of Collective Action.* Cambridge: Harvard University Press.

Owen, Bruce M., and Ronald Braeutigam. 1978. *The Regulation Game: Strategic Use of the Administrative Process.* Cambridge: Ballinger Publishing Co.

Paglin, Max D. 1989. *A Legislative History of the Communications Act of 1934.* Oxford: Oxford University Press.

Polenberg, Richard. 1966. *Reorganizing Roosevelt's Government: The Controversy over Executive Reorganization, 1936–1939.* Cambridge: Harvard University Press.

Polsby, Nelson. 1968. "The Institutionalization of the U.S. House of Representatives." *American Political Science Review* 62:144–68.

Posner, Richard. 1985. *The Federal Courts.* Cambridge: Harvard University Press.

Pritchett, C. Herman. 1948. *The Roosevelt Court.* New York: MacMillan.

Rabin, Robert L. 1975. "Preclusion of Judicial Review in the Processing of Claims for Veterans' Benefits: A Preliminary Analysis." *Stanford Law Review* 27:905–23.

———. 1986. "Federal Regulation in Historical Perspective." *Stanford Law Review* 38:1189–1326.

Radio Corporation of America. 1922. *Annual Report of the Directors for the Year Ended December 31, 1922.* New York: RCA.

Rashkow, Ilona N. 1976. "Judicial Review for Veterans' Claims." CRS Report for Congress, June 18. Washington, DC: Library of Congress.

Reck, Franklin M. 1942. *Radio From Start to Finish.* New York: Thomas Y. Crowell Co.

Richardson, Richard J., and Kenneth N. Vines. 1970. *The Politics of Federal Courts.* Boston: Little, Brown.

Robinson, Glen O. 1989a. "The Federal Communications Act: An Essay on Origins and Regulatory Purpose." In *A Legislative History of the Communications Act of 1934,* ed. Max D. Paglin. Oxford: Oxford University Press.

———. 1989b. "Commentary on 'Administrative Arrangements and the Political Control of Agencies': Political Uses of Structure and Process." *Virginia Law Review* 75:483–98.

Robinson, Thomas Porter. 1943. *Radio Networks and the Federal Government.* New York: Columbia University Press.

Rohde, David W., and Harold J. Spaeth. 1976. *Supreme Court Decision Making.* San Francisco: W. H. Freeman.

Rose-Ackerman, Susan. 1992. *Rethinking the Progressive Agenda.* New York: Free Press.

Rosen, Philip T. 1980. *The Modern Stentors: Radio Broadcasters and the Federal Government, 1920–1934.* Westport, CT: Greenwood Press.

Rosenberg, Gerald. 1991. *The Hollow Hope.* Chicago: University of Chicago Press.

Russell, Peter H. 1991. "The Diffusion of Judicial Review: The Commonwealth, the United States, and the Canadian Case." *Policy Studies Journal* 19 (1): 116–26.

Schlesinger, Arthur M., Jr. 1958. *The Coming of the New Deal.* Boston: Houghton Mifflin.

Schlozman, Kay Lehman, and John T. Tierney. 1986. *Organized Interests and American Democracy.* New York: Harper and Row.

Schmeckebier, Lawrence F. 1932. *The Federal Radio Commission: Its History, Activities, and Organization.* Washington, DC: Brookings Institution.

Schubert, Glendon. 1965. *The Judicial Mind.* Evanston, IL: Northwestern University Press.

Segal, Jeffrey A. 1995. "Marksist (and Neo-Marksist) Models of Supreme Court Decision Making: Separation-of-Powers Games in the Positive Theory of Law and Courts." Paper presented at the annual meeting of the American Political Science Association, Chicago, August 30–September 3.

Segal, Jeffrey A., Charles M. Cameron, and Albert D. Cover. 1992. "A Spatial Model of Roll Call Voting: Senators, Constituents, Presidents, and Interest Groups in Supreme Court Confirmations." *American Journal of Political Science* 36:96–121.

Segal, Jeffrey A., and Albert D. Cover. 1989. "Ideological Values and the Votes of U.S. Supreme Court Justices." *American Political Science Review* 83: 557–565.

Segal, Jeffrey A., and Harold J. Spaeth. 1993. *The Supreme Court and the Attitudinal Model.* New York: Cambridge University Press.

Seidman, Baruch S. 1934. "The Communications Act of 1934." *Air Law Review* 5:299–306.

Severin, Werner J. 1978. "Commercial v. Non-Commercial Radio During Broadcasting's Early Years." *Journal of Broadcasting* 22 (4): 491–504.

Shapiro, Martin. 1968. *The Supreme Court and Administrative Agencies.* New York: Free Press.

———. 1982. "On Predicting the Future of Administrative Law." *Regulation* (May–June): 18–25.

———. 1988. *Who Guards the Guardians?* Athens, GA: University of Georgia Press.

Shepsle, Kenneth. 1990. "Congress is a 'They,' not an 'It': Legislative Intent as Oxymoron." Harvard University: Center for American Political Studies, Occasion Paper 90–8.

———. 1992. "Bureaucratic Drift, Coalitional Drift, and Time Consistency: A Comment on Macey." *Journal of Law, Economics, and Organization* 8:111–25.

Shipan, Charles R. 1992. "Interest Groups and Provisions for Judicial Review." Paper presented at the annual meeting of the American Political Science Association, Chicago, September 3–6.

———. 1993. "Judicial Review as a Political Variable: Interest Groups, Congress, and Communications Policy." Ph.D. diss., Stanford University.

———. 1995. "Is there an Americanist Bias in Organization Theory?" *Governance* 8 (1): 125–34.

———. 1996. "Senate Committees and Turf: Do Jurisdictions Matter?" *Political Research Quarterly* 49 (1): 177–89.

———. 1997 (forthcoming). "Interest Groups, Judicial Review, and the Origins of Broadcasting Regulation." *Administrative Law Review.*

Simon, Herbert A. 1957. *Administrative Behavior,* 2d ed. New York: MacMillan.

Skowronek, Stephen. 1982. *Building a New American State.* Cambridge: Cambridge University Press.

Smith, Joseph, and Emerson H. Tiller. 1996. "The Strategy of Judging: An Empirical Assessment." Paper presented at the annual meeting of the Midwest Political Science Association, Chicago, April 18–20.

Smulyan, Susan. 1994. *Selling Radio.* Washington, DC: Smithsonian Press.

Songer, Donald R., Jeffrey A. Segal, and Charles M. Cameron. 1994. "The Hierarchy of Justice: Testing a Principal-Agent Model of Supreme Court–Circuit Court Interactions." *American Journal of Political Science* 38 (3): 673–96.

Sorauf, Frank J. 1976. *The Wall of Separation: Constitutional Politics of Church and State.* Princeton: Princeton University Press.

Spiller, Pablo T. 1992a. Rationality, Decision Rules, and Collegial Courts." *International Review of Law and Economics* 12 (2): 186–90.

———. 1992b. "Agency Discretion under Judicial Review." *Mathematical and Computer Modeling* 16:185–94.

Spiller, Pablo T., and Rafael Gely. 1992. "Congressional Control or Judicial Independence: The Determinants of U.S. Supreme Court Labor Relations Decisions, 1949/1988." *RAND Journal of Economics* 23:463–92.

Spiller, Pablo T., and Emerson H. Tiller. 1996. "Decision Costs and the Strategic Design of Judicial Review and Administrative Processes." Paper presented at the annual meeting of the American Political Science Association, San Francisco, August 28–September 1.

Spitzer, Matthew L. 1990. "Extensions of Ferejohn and Shipan's Model of Administrative Agency Behavior." *Journal of Law, Economics, and Organization* 6: 29–43.

Sterling, Christopher H., and John M. Kittross. 1990. *Stay Tuned,* 2d ed. Belmont, CA: Wadsworth Publishing Co.

Stewart, Richard. 1975. "The Reformation of American Administrative Law." *Harvard Law Review* 88:1669–1813.

Stigler, George. 1971. "The Theory of Economic Regulation." *Bell Journal of Economics and Management Science* 2:3–21.

Stone, Alan. 1991. *Public Service Liberalism: Telecommunications and Transitions in Public Policy.* Princeton: Princeton University Press.

Temin, Peter. 1987. *The Fall of the Bell System.* Cambridge: Cambridge University Press.

Thernstrom, Abigail M. 1987. *Whose Votes Count? Affirmative Action and Minority Voting Rights.* Cambridge: Harvard University Press.

Truman, David B. 1951. *The Governmental Process.* New York: Knopf.

Tushnet, Mark V. 1987. *Red, White, and Blue.* Cambridge: Harvard University Press.

Ulloth, Dana Royal. 1979. *The Supreme Court: A Judicial Review of the Federal Communications Commission.* New York: Arno Press.

Ulmer, Sidney S. 1984. "The Supreme Court's Certiorari Decisions: Conflict as a Predictive Variable." *American Political Science Review* 78:901–11.

U.S. House. 1958. Committee on Interstate and Foreign Commerce. *Regulation of Broadcasting: Half a Century of Government Regulation of Broadcasting and the Need For Further Legislative Action.* 85th Cong., 2d session.

Vose, Clement E. 1959. *Caucasians Only.* Berkeley: University of California Press.

Warner, Harry P. 1940. "Subjective Judicial Review of the Federal Communications Commission." *Michigan Law Review* 38:632–80.

Weaver, R. Kent. 1986. "The Politics of Blame Avoidance." *Journal of Public Policy* 6 (October–December): 371–98.

Weaver, Suzanne. 1980. "Antitrust Division of the Department of Justice." In *The Politics of Regulation,* ed. James Q. Wilson. New York: Basic Books.

Weingast, Barry R., and William Marshall. 1988. "The Industrial Organization of Congress: or, Why Legislatures, Like Firms, Are Not Organized as Markets." *Journal of Political Economy* 96 (1): 132–63.

Weingast, Barry R., and Mark J. Moran. 1983. "Bureaucratic Discretion or Congressional Control: Regulatory Policymaking by the FTC." *Journal of Political Economy* 91:765–800.

West, William. 1985. *Administrative Rulemaking: Politics and Process.* Westport, CT: Greenwood Press.

Weyland, Kurt. 1995. "The Americanist Bias in Organization." *Governance* 8 (1): 113–24.

White, Llewellyn. 1947. *The American Radio.* Chicago: University of Chicago Press.

Williams, Robert J. 1977. "The Politics of American Broadcasting: Public Purposes and Private Interests." *American Studies* 10 (3): 329–40.

Wilson, James Q. 1980. *The Politics of Regulation.* New York: Basic Books.

———. 1985. "Neglected Areas of Research on Regulation." In *Regulatory Policy and the Social Sciences,* ed. Roger G. Noll. Berkeley: University of California Press.

———. 1990. *Bureaucracy.* New York: Basic Books.

Wolfe, Christopher. 1994. *The Rise of Modern Judicial Review,* rev. ed. Lanham, MD: Littlefield Adams Quality Paperbacks.

Wonnacutt, Thomas H., and Ronald J. Wonnacutt. 1984. *Introductory Statistics for Business and Economics,* 3d ed. New York: John Wiley and Sons.

Author Index

Subject Index